THE
FIGHT
FOR
MARRIAGE

Praise for *The Fight for Marriage*

"The story of how deep faith and belief in 'the sacred worth and dignity of all God's children' galvanized the professional trajectories of two lawyers, emboldened their congregation, and set them on the path towards justice in the church and in the law of the land."
—Patricia Farris, Senior Minister, First UMC of Santa Monica, Santa Monica, CA

"Cramer and Harbison remind us that marriage is a sacred contract—a solemn vow—rooted in God's covenant, not our gender. The sooner we acknowledge this in the church, the better we will bear witness to the depth of God's love and the breadth of its expression by all people."
—Steve Harper, author, retired seminary professor and United Methodist elder

"An amazing story, which I could not put down, of the flight all the way to the Supreme Court and the journey of their congregation coming out in support of same-sex marriage. A powerful story of faith enacted to promote social justice."
—Michael Regele, CEO, MissionInsite; author, *Science, Scripture, and Same-Sex Love*

THE FIGHT FOR MARRIAGE

CHURCH CONFLICTS AND COURTROOM CONTESTS

PHILLIP F. CRAMER AND WILLIAM L. HARBISON

Abingdon Press™
Nashville

THE FIGHT FOR MARRIAGE:
CHURCH CONFLICTS AND COURTROOM CONTESTS

Copyright © 2018 by Abingdon Press

All rights reserved.

This book is printed on acid-free paper.

Library of Congress Cataloging-in-Publication Data has been requested.

ISBN: 978-1-5018-5893-2

The photograph on page 21 is © Mike BuBose.

The photograph on page 96 is © Pamela Hawkins.

All other interior photographs are © Patricia Harbison.

18 19 20 21 22 23 24 25 26 27—10 9 8 7 6 5 4 3 2 1
MANUFACTURED IN THE UNITED STATES OF AMERICA

CONTENTS

DEDICATION

We dedicate this book to our spouses. Our journeys within the courts and our church made us realize how much we had taken for granted our ability to marry the person we each loved. We just had to ask. And perhaps the manner in we each asked our respective spouses to marry us foretold that we would one day be on a journey to the Supreme Court.

Thirty-eight years ago, while Bill was a law student at Harvard, he presented an engagement ring to his future spouse, Patty, in the Harvard moot courtroom, where Bill had competed in the school-wide moot court competition. Bill would return to the appellate courtroom decades later to argue for the right of all persons to have the same ability he had to ask the love of his life to marry him.

Phil asked his future spouse, Anna, to marry him on the steps of the Supreme Court. They were entering their second year of law school and Phil and Anna were in Washington, DC, to attend the wedding of Phil's childhood friend. Under the guise of visiting the Supreme Court, Phil got down on his knees to propose as they stood on the steps of the Supreme Court. It would be the same steps that we would walk down seventeen years later with our same-gender couple plaintiffs after one of the most significant civil rights cases in our generation.

We also dedicate this book to our entire families, including our respective children Jay, Clare, and Jane Coleman, and Caroline, Lucy, and Alice. They have been our inspiration to step outside our comfort zones and place our faith into action. We also have such gratitude for our law partners, Scott Hickman and John Farringer, with whom we journeyed to the Supreme Court along with every member of the Tennessee marriage equality team, including Shannon Minter, David Codell, and Chris Stoll of the National Center for Lesbian Rights (NCLR), Douglas Hallward-Driemier and Tom Brown of Ropes and Gray, and of course Abby Rubenfeld, Mauren Holland, and Regina Lambert. We also dedicate this book to the courageous couples who trusted us with the privilege of telling their story all the way to the Supreme Court: Valeria Tanco and Sophy Jesty, Matthew Mansell and Johno Espejo, and Ijpe DeKoe and Thom Kostura. Finally, we dedicate this book to our entire church family at Belmont United Methodist Church and our many personal heroes whom we have been fortunate to befriend at our church, past and present, including the dedicated lay leaders, Sunday school class members, the individual beacons for hope and justice, the beloved pastoral staff, and Reverend Pam Hawkins who risked her pastoral career to fulfill her ordination vows.

1

THE POWER OF
THE NARRATIVE

When a child is baptized in The United Methodist Church, the parents or sponsors of the child are asked to affirm whether they "accept the freedom and power God gives you to resist evil, injustice, and oppression in whatever forms they present themselves." What does it mean to accept the freedom and power given by God? What happens when injustice or oppression takes the form of the state? Or the church itself? And how does one "live according to the example of Christ" and serve Jesus Christ "in union with the Church" when the church itself is not unified?

This book traces our attempts to answer these questions in the context of marriage equality. The story is told from the perspective of two United Methodists—lay leaders and lawyers—who live in two coexisting and overlapping worlds: the church and the state. In those overlapping worlds we simultaneously represented same-gender couples seeking recognition of their marriages by the state, while working within our local congregation as it sought acceptance of LGBTQ persons in the eyes of

The United Methodist Church. While the perspective is ours, the stories are not.

In our professional lives, we are charged to give voice to those who need to be heard within our legal system. While we do so within the technical and specialized environment that constitutes the American legal system, we are actually packaging the underlying narratives. And these narratives are the essence of what conveys truth.

In many ways, our professional lives are modeled after our faith tradition in which laws and principles are often more effectively conveyed by stories or parables than by edicts or pronouncements. While some principles can be expressed through simple commandants such as "thou shall not kill," other principles require narratives to explain and understand. Jesus frequently used parables to express deep and compelling truths. For example, one does not place a lamp under a bowl or build on ground without a foundation. And it is the smallest of all seeds, the mustard seed, that when planted becomes the largest of all garden plants. Or it is the one lost sheep that is found that creates more happiness than the ninety-nine sheep that did not wander off. And it is not just the stories told by Jesus but also the stories about Jesus that have been used within our faith tradition to express a way of life. For example, the story of Jesus casting out the demons from Legion conveyed significant political and social commentary on multiple levels that would have been readily understood at the time.

Our journey as storytellers is deeply rooted in our faith. A faith that compelled us to action and action that required our faith. It is a faith grounded in the kingdom of God, experienced right here and right now. This faith has confidence in both the church and the law. And it is a faith in and exercised through the power of the narrative.

Our interest in taking action against inequality is rooted in our own stories. Why would we want to take on a case about marriage? Lawyers are affected and changed by the cases they take and the life experiences that they encounter. The fact that marriage was available in Tennessee to opposite-gender couples, but not to same-gender couples, was, to us, unjust. Things from our past reminded us of that injustice and compelled us to act.

In the early 1980s, Bill worked on a dispute between Yale University in New Haven and Fisk University in Nashville about the ownership of the unpublished papers of Jean Toomer, a renowned author of the Harlem Renaissance. Jean Toomer's widow, Marjorie Content Toomer, lived in Doylestown, Pennsylvania, and Bill was sent to interview her about the case.

The nature of the dispute about Jean Toomer's papers is not relevant to what happened next. Bill arrived in Doylestown and rented a car, finding his way by maps to Marjorie Toomer's home in an old renovated barn just outside of town. The house was filled with original paintings, furniture, and the collections of an interesting life. Marjorie was in her eighties, and offered a drink of Jack Daniel's. Jean Toomer had died many years earlier. As Marjorie discussed her life and her intentions about his literary legacy, she brought out a New York newspaper clipping from the 1930s with this headline: "Miss Content Marries a Negro." The couple was legally allowed to marry in New York (although it drew this type of headline, even in that state), but that marriage would have been unlawful in Tennessee (and many other states) in the 1930s.

The memory of that headline remains as a reminder of how unfairly people are sometimes treated for reasons that have nothing to do with their basic human dignity or sacred worth. Of all the memories that Bill heard from Marjorie that day, over the course of several hours, this was one that she had preserved and wanted to show as an explanation of a portion of her life. She became a real friend that day. Bill and his wife, Patty, were expecting their first child, Jay, who was born later that year. Marjorie sent them a sweater for Jay that she had knitted by hand.

Phil was likewise profoundly affected by his own life experiences as a young attorney. Phil's daughter Caroline was celebrating her fourth birthday, which happened to fall on Martin Luther King Jr. Day. As he tucked his daughter into bed that evening, he read to her a children's book about MLK's boyhood. It had capped a day of remembrance and awareness that included a family ritual of watching King's "I Have a Dream" speech around the breakfast table.

When Phil finished reading the book to his daughter, he decided to use it as a parental teaching moment. He explained to his young child that injustice and inequality persisted to this day and she had a responsibility to take action. Before Phil could pat himself on the back for instilling this bit of parental wisdom, the teaching moment was turned on its head. His daughter looked him in the eyes and asked, innocently and sincerely as only young children can do, "Daddy, so what are you doing?" This question would ring in Phil's ears in the coming days, weeks, and months as he worked at our business law firm. And it would be a turning point for Phil to remember why he went to law school in the first place.

Years after these experiences, in late April 2015, we both were together in Washington, DC, for one of the most significant cases in which we could ever imagine to participate. Other members of our law firm, and other members of the legal team of which we were a part, were also in Washington that week. On Tuesday, April 28, 2015, the US Supreme Court would hear arguments in the case of *Obergefell v. Hodges*, a consolidated case that presented the court with questions about whether same-gender couples have the right to marry, and to have their marriages recognized in all fifty states. Our Tennessee case was part of that consolidated case.

That night, however, was a moment of calm before the big event in the Supreme Court. Legal briefs had been written and submitted, and preparation was nearing completion. The rest of our legal team had plans for the evening, and so the two of us walked from our hotel in search of a restaurant. We found a charming French restaurant a few blocks away that had an open table. It was a beautiful night, and we were seated on the restaurant's patio. At the next table, two other men sat together and the waiter was delivering their appetizers. Our table neighbors were friendly, and they made suggestions for us to consider ordering. They lived nearby, and were familiar with the menu.

A little further into the meal, they asked what brought us to Washington. We explained that we were lawyers from Tennessee, and that we were there for the Supreme Court case on marriage. Warily, they asked us which side we represented. When we told them that we represented the plaintiffs seeking legal recognition of their marriages, they beamed with pleasure and told us that they were themselves a committed couple. Our lives and stories were intersecting at a moment in time that was hugely significant for all of us.

How we reached that moment, and what happened after, has formed our perspective on marriage equality.

2

THE MARCH TOWARD EQUALITY WITHIN MARRIAGE

Marriage is a unique creation. It is about love and loyalty. It is part contract and part covenant. It has the power to make life convenient while adding untold complexity, often simultaneously. It is expected by society yet historically made exclusive. And it is arguably the only institution in the United States that transcends both civil law and church doctrine.

That was not always the case. Under Roman law, marriage was a civil institution that included various types of partnership arrangements that evolved during the Roman Republic and the Roman Empire that followed. The types of marriage available to Roman citizens and subjects were typically dictated by the class of the individuals involved. Roman law dictated the rights of the spouses both during and after marriage; these rights were largely about property, especially for the more wealthy families during Roman times.

In the world in which Jesus was born, marriage was primarily an economic contract and social compact. And while for some marriage had roots in the Jewish faith, its purpose was viewed in largely secular and societal terms around order, property rights, and economic stability. Consider, for example, Proverbs 31, which is still used today as scripture at weddings. While the passage includes flowery language about a wife whose "husband praises her" and whose "children bless her," to young women of the day it read more like a job description of a virtuous wife.

Church and State

The relationship between the church and state with respect to marriage has been both complementary and antagonistic. For example, when Augustus ushered in the Roman Empire, civil marriage had fallen out of favor and Rome faced declining birth rates. Augustus sought to impose strict laws governing marriage requiring that all men between twenty-five and sixty years of age and all women between twenty and fifty were to marry and have children. Roman couples who declined to have children were taxed proportionally by their wealth. Those who engaged in adultery would be exiled, if they were not killed by either a father or husband. It was the early church that opposed such laws and had success in securing their repeal or lack of enforcement.

Indeed, many early Christian communities discouraged marriage because it distracted followers from the Way. Of course, they recognized that a community that solely promoted celibacy would not remain very long. Marriage began to receive more acceptance from early Christians after it was suggested by some that it was a sacrament; after all, why else would Jesus turn water into wine at a wedding? However, marriage would not become an official sacrament (a sign of divine grace) in the Catholic Church for more than a millennium.

As Christianity and Christian communities grew, the church found itself having to address the marriage practices of those who were being brought into the faith. For example, polygamy was practiced within many communities that converted to Christianity. The church did not prohibit clerical polygamy until the eighth century. During the centuries that followed, the church had an uneasy relationship with marriage, because it was used by the powerful and elite as both a saber and a sword, often with the church's complicity.

During the sixteenth century, the church (which now included both Catholics and Protestants) reexamined the sacramental nature of marriage. During the seventh session of the Council of Trent in 1547, sacramental marriage became part of Roman Catholic canon law. The adoption of sacramental marriage as part of the canon law was as much about recognizing the importance of marriage as it was an attempt to influence, if not dictate, centuries of civil law and customs over the practice of marriage.

An Unequal Union

Under both civil law and canonical law, marriage was historically an unequal arrangement. Males assumed the head of the household and females were often regarded as property instead of coequal partners. It was not uncommon under civil law for the property rights of the wife to be transferred from her family to her husband. It was the wife's duty to "obey" while the husband was obliged to "honor." For example, marriage vows from the mid-sixteenth century in the Church of England had the groom promising to "love, cherish, and worship" while the wife vowed to "love, cherish, and obey."

This understanding of marriage, with its inherent inequity of those in the relationship, continued for centuries and became part of civil law. In nineteenth-century America, the law insisted that marriage was a permanent relationship defined by the husband's authority and the wife's dependence. These laws governed property rights, obligation and right to support, legal ability to contract, and the inheritance rights of offspring. These laws have components of both earlier Roman civil law and religious doctrinal teachings.

One can trace the evolution and understanding of marriage from Roman civil law to church doctrinal law and then back to American civil law. An in-depth history of marriage is beyond the scope of this book; the important takeaway, however, is that the institution of marriage has looked different at different points in time, and the relationship between church and state with respect to marriage has been anything but static throughout the millennia.

Similarly, the reasons for marriage have evolved over time. Marriage has served as an instrument to combine and preserve power and wealth, especially among politically elevated families. On the opposite end of the spectrum, marriage offered stability and security facilitating the potential for economic advancement. And of course, marriage has served as a platform for the mutual expression of love and affection.

The institution of marriage has reflected the societies of the time while simultaneously shaping those societies. This symbiotic relationship has played itself out in American society over the past century. Perhaps the most fundamental change in American society over the past one hundred years has been the greater recognition and deeper understanding of individual rights. Races are no longer viewed as unequal. Women are no longer viewed as property. And all persons, regardless of sexual orientation, are recognized as having equal dignity.

These changes in our relationships and regard for the equal dignity of all persons has meant that while marriage remains a combination of two persons, the recognition of the rights of those persons within the marriage has evolved. While marriage continues to be a combination of two individuals, the opportunities to marry and the worth of those within the marriage are now equal.

Sacred and Equal Worth

Today, most Christian faith communities embrace the sacred worth of all persons, either as a tenet of faith or as a commandment. This expectation itself has evolved. While the Bible has numerous passages and parables preaching equality and love for all, other passages have been used throughout history to support separation and inequality, including the unequal treatment of women and minorities. Indeed, the Judeo-Christian tradition has an unfortunate and ugly history of using scripture to support separation, slavery, and submissiveness of groups based on skin color, skin disease, ethnic origin, or gender. However, during the past one hundred years, the church has, more often than not, been at the forefront of promoting equality, and most Christian faith communities today fully embrace the sacred worth of all individuals.

American civil law has likewise evolved to embrace a notion of equality for all. Like the church, the founding of the American experiment was a paradox of lofty statements about equality and human dignity undermined by discriminatory practices and laws. Races were separated and subjugated. Genders were categorized and casted. Although the phrase "Equal Justice Under Law" was carved in stone above the entrance of the Supreme Court building in Washington, DC, when it was completed in 1935, equality for all was still an elusive idea. Over the past 150 years, we have seen the abolishment of slavery, the elimination of Jim Crow laws, the enshrinement of equal protection in the US Constitution, the extension of universal suffrage, and the enactment of protections for women, minorities, the disabled, and the disenfranchised.

While both the church and civil law have moved toward embracing dignity for all, its leaders have not always been proactive in updating the institutions that they created or sponsored to incorporate such ideals. And therein lies the challenge. It is a process that has repeated itself from the founding of both the Christian church and the American state. Implementation of policy frequently lags behind proclamation of ideals. This delay and resistance is similar to the tension between faith and works. What does one tell us of the other, especially when what we profess and preach is not always represented by our actions? Is the resistance an indictment of our professed beliefs or actually failing to act as we believe? And given that both civil law and church law are distinctly human institutions subject to the will of those in power, they become a proxy for larger disagreements within society and faith communities.

Sacred Sign

Perhaps no institution has become more of a proxy for larger disagreements within society and faith communities in recent years than marriage. And for good reason. The importance of marriage as an institution to both the church and state cannot be overstated. In American society today, marriage embodies an expression of emotional support and public commitment that carry both spiritual significance and societal status, including the receipt of government benefits and property rights. The United States Supreme Court affirmed in 1978 that "the right to marry is of fundamental importance for all individuals," and one that "has long been recognized as one of the vital personal rights essential to the orderly pursuit of happiness." Modern civil law in the United States recognizes that for many, marriage is "the most important relation in life." It is a relationship conferring dignity and status, and serving many functions, among them protection of the couple and of any children they rear.

The overlap between civil law and church doctrine is exemplified by how the US Supreme Court describes marriage: "a coming together for better or for worse, hopefully enduring, and intimate to the degree of being sacred." Civilly, the freedom to marry is protected by the US Constitution because the intimate relationship a person forms with a spouse, and the decision whether to formalize such a relationship through marriage, implicate deeply held personal beliefs and core values. As the Supreme Court has affirmed, "Family relationships, by their nature, involve deep attachments and commitments to the necessarily few other individuals with whom one shares not only a special community of thoughts, experiences, and beliefs but also distinctively personal aspects of one's life."

Faith communities have made similar pronouncements about the importance of marriage from a religious perspective. The Catholic Church regards marriage as one of its seven sacraments. Although marriage is not a sacrament in The United Methodist Church, the second-largest Protestant denomination, it is "a sacred covenant reflecting the Baptismal Covenant" and "Christ's covenant with the church." The United Methodist Church "affirm[s] the sanctity of the marriage covenant that is expressed in love, mutual support, personal commitment, and shared fidelity." The Southern Baptist Convention, the largest Protestant denomination, describes the family "as the foundational institution of human society," which is "composed of persons related to one another by marriage, blood or adoption." Marriage is a "covenant commitment for a lifetime." According to the Presbyterian Church (USA), "Marriage is a gift God has given to all human kind for the wellbeing of the entire human family." The Presbyterian Church (USA) *Book of Order* explains the relationship between the church and state when it comes to marriage: "In civil law, marriage is a contract that recognizes the rights and obligations of the married couple in society. In the Reformed tradition, marriage is also a covenant in which God has an active part, and which the community of faith publicly witnesses and acknowledges."

Although marriage has changed over time, to most people in both the church and the state, it is loaded with their own concepts of what has always been. While the church and the state have a dual and sometimes dueling interest in marriage in present-day society, they are both guided (and hampered) by "tradition." Within the church, tradition is at times omnipresent. It is present in our prayers and our practices. Tradition binds together generations. Tradition is sometimes tantamount to faith. And it is a source for our theological views. This is especially true in The United Methodist Church, which was influenced by John Wesley to base theological conclusions on scripture, tradition, reason, and Christian practices. According to Wesley, traditional evidence should have "its place and its due honour," and links our faith history back to Jesus and the apostles. However, even Wesley acknowledged that traditional evidence is weakened by length of time.

Civil law is also rooted in tradition. The very practice of law is steeped in tradition and ritual practices. However, like the Wesleyans, courts recognize that tradition cannot alone control. This is especially true in the area of civil rights, in which the concept of "tradition" is often invoked by the oppressor against those historically oppressed. The US Supreme Court makes plain that the "[a]ncient lineage of a legal concept does not give it immunity from attack."

Both the state and many Christian churches recognize equality among all people, regardless of gender. This is a relatively recent phenomenon and a break from past practices or tradition. Historically, marriage under both civil and church law treated women differently. For centuries, it was commonly understood that a married woman had no legal personality separate from that of her husband. Throughout much of the nineteenth century, married women were denied the legal capacity to hold or convey property or to serve as legal guardians of their own children. Under the principles of coverture, a married woman was incapable of making a binding contract without her spouse's consent. Likewise, a wife could not be party to a lawsuit without her spouse's consent, and husbands were solely responsible for providing economic support. Even well into the twentieth century, spousal rape was largely not considered a crime, reflecting an acceptance of the idea that the marriage constituted a blanket consent to sexual intimacy that the woman could revoke only by dissolving the marital relationship.

Laws pertaining to the marriage relationship have since developed to eliminate virtually every vestige of such disparate treatment and historical gender roles. However, Tennessee did not explicitly abolish the doctrine of coverture until the 1970s, in a state Supreme Court decision in which Bill's father participated as one of the justices of that court. Today, a combination of constitutional sex-discrimination adjudication, legislative changes, and social and cultural transformation has sought to eliminate legal gender-based distinctions in marriage. Married women and married men may own property, enter into contracts, work in professions, sue and be sued, and otherwise act independently of their spouses. Spouses are entitled to economic support regardless of gender, and the same is true of child and spousal support in case of divorce. In addition, men and women are guaranteed legal equality with respect to children.

Church law has undergone a similar transformation. The United Methodist Church has "reject[ed] social norms that assume different standards for women than for men in marriage." And Southern Baptists believe that spouses "are of equal worth before God," albeit having separate obligations. Even the Catholic Church teaches that while women are to be valued for certain unique qualities within a marriage, as individuals, men and women are of equal worth within marriage.

Interracial Marriage

The role of tradition in both the church and civil law is also exemplified by how both institutions addressed interracial marriage. While the Catholic Church never prohibited interracial marriage, it has long had concerns about interfaith marriages. Protestant churches, especially in the United States, have a history of prohibiting interracial marriage. Even into this century, some churches and religious institutions, including schools, prohibited not just interracial marriage but also interracial dating. While such prohibitions had their roots in discrimination, they had their justification in "tradition."

American civil law has a long history of prohibiting interracial marriage under the guise of tradition. Indeed, three separate attempts were made to amend the US Constitution to forever memorialize such "traditions" that were already codified in many states' laws. And while such laws are now largely associated with the Deep South, the South was not the only place that legally barred interracial marriage. Indeed, California had its ban until 1948. These civil laws, like their religious counterparts, were justified by tradition.

At the time of the Supreme Court's 1967 decision in *Loving v. Virginia*, which overturned Virginia's ban on interracial marriage, the "traditional" definition of marriage in Virginia and many other states was an institution restricted to two persons of the same race or, more insidiously, of two white persons or two non-white persons. The Supreme Court in *Loving* nonetheless determined that even though the governing majority in Virginia and similar states had traditionally viewed a particular practice as immoral, such tradition was not sufficient basis for upholding a law prohibiting the practice; neither history nor tradition could save a law prohibiting interracial marriage from constitutional attack.

Same-Gender Marriage

Prohibitions in both civil and church law on marriage between persons of the same gender have likewise been rooted in tradition. Even though civil laws prohibiting marriage between persons of the same gender are relatively recent, with Maryland enacting the first such prohibition in 1973, the basis for such prohibitions draws on history. Indeed, most states had no laws on their books prohibiting marriage between persons of the same gender because the very concept had never been raised or attempted civilly. However, when the Hawaii Supreme Court ruled in 1993 that the state could not deny same-gender couples the right to marry unless the state legislature could demonstrate a compelling reason to do so, a wave of states and the federal government rushed to enact legislation and even constitutional amendments prohibiting both the recognition and right of same-gender marriage.

The states were not alone in their reaction. Churches took action too. The reaction of the Southern Baptist Convention illustrates the relationship between the church and the state with respect to marriage. By 2003, Vermont had embraced civil unions of same-gender couples, and a handful of other states were considering similar arrangements. The Southern Baptist Convention responded with a resolution in which it recited developments in Vermont, California, Massachusetts, and New Jersey along with marriage equality in Belgium and Holland and the prospect of court challenges to state and federal government Defense of Marriage Acts as the basis for resolving and affirming "that legal and biblical marriage can only occur between one man and one woman."

The resolution further declared that the Southern Baptist Convention will "continue to oppose steadfastly all efforts by any court or state legislature to validate or legalize same-sex marriage or other equivalent unions" and "to pray for and support legislative and legal efforts to oppose the legalization of same-sex unions." The resolution went so far as to "call upon all judges and public officials to resist and oppose the legalization of same-sex unions." In passing this resolution, the Southern Baptist Convention readily demonstrates the interrelationship between church and state with respect to the institution of marriage. Interestingly, the Baptist tradition was founded upon a firm separation of church and state, dating to a time when Baptist followers were oppressed and killed by other Christian believers.

The history of same-gender marriage within The United Methodist Church parallels the history within the states. At its founding quadrennial General Conference in 1972, The United Methodist Church added language to its governing *Book of Discipline* stating: "We do not condone the practice of homosexuality and consider it incompatible with Christian teaching." In addition to addressing sexual orientation for the first time in Methodist governing documents, The United Methodist Church also added language to its Social Principles stating that "we do not recommend marriage between two persons of the same sex." At the next General Conference in 1976, this language was revised to state, "We do not recognize a relationship between two persons of the same sex as constituting marriage." It was further revised in 1980 to provide that "we affirm the sanctity of the marriage covenant, which is expressed in love, mutual support, personal commitment, and shared fidelity between a man and woman." This language would be affirmed at every subsequent General Conference of the church, with the adoption of an absolute prohibition in 1996 on any ceremonies to celebrate same gender unions by United Methodist clergy or in United Methodist churches.

Both within The United Methodist Church and within the states themselves, each effort to prohibit same-gender marriage was met with persons who opposed such prohibitions. For example, United Methodists organized under various banners, including the Reconciling Ministries Network, to oppose each additional prohibition to *The Book of Discipline* and to remove the prohibitions that were added. The roots of the Reconciling Ministries Network trace back to 1982 at a meeting of Affirmation: United Methodists for Lesbian/Gay Concerns in Boston. The idea was broached of modeling the More Light Program, which had begun in 1979 by the Presbyterians for Lesbian and Gay Concerns. By the end of 1984, nine congregations identified as Reconciling Congregations. By 2017, 865 faith communities identify as Reconciling.

This book is not meant to be a history of the struggle for marriage equality within The United Methodist Church or any other church. Nor is it meant to be an exhaustive history of the legal case for marriage equality within the fifty states and federal government. Those efforts span decades and involve people who were far more instrumental than we and who worked far longer. The stories we experienced are, however, part of that larger story, and we happened to be two of the lawyers fortunate enough to be involved in the case that ended up before the US Supreme Court. However, our involvement with marriage equality did not start in the courtroom. Rather, it began in our church.

3

TOGETHER AND APART

We are both members of Belmont United Methodist Church in Nashville, Tennessee, although our paths to the church could not be more different. Bill grew up attending Belmont, where a Sunday school class remains named after his father, in whose footsteps Bill followed in teaching both children and adults. By contrast, Phil is the son of a former Catholic nun and would find his way to United Methodism decades later as a result of his marriage. Belmont Methodist Episcopal Church, South, was founded in 1910, in response to the expanding population center of Nashville that was moving away from the center of town along the river. Ground was broken by the Tennessee Conference in the Hillsboro Village section of town for a new church building. Belmont Methodist Episcopal Church was founded at the same time the larger Methodist movement was embracing the church's role in society. The General Conference of The Methodist Episcopal Church first adopted its Social Principles in 1908. The Methodist Episcopal Church, South, would follow suit in 1914.

As Nashville burgeoned and the church's outward look grew, Belmont Methodist Church took shape. The church exhibited early support for mission activities throughout the world, including Asia and Africa. This continued through two world wars and the Great Depression. Belmont's mission work came into sharper focus after World War II, with support for several missionaries throughout Asia and support for the people of Japan immediately after the end of the war.

Despite Belmont's global reach and support for persons of different races and ethnicities abroad, the church struggled internally with inclusion. In 1948, one section of the balcony was set aside for African Americans; however, and not surprisingly, none chose to attend under such segregated circumstances. The congregation held differing views regarding integration and inclusiveness. This divide would come to a head in the mid-1950s. In 1954, a request was made to allow the church building to host a meeting of students from African American colleges; the request was denied by an ad hoc group of Belmont members. In 1956, the governing body of the church, the administrative board, formally petitioned the senior pastor, John Rustin, to sign a statement pledging that he would not receive an African American member into the membership of the church. After John Rustin refused the board's request, some Belmont worshipers moved their membership in protest.

According to the *History of Belmont*, "as racial tension mounted in the community and the nation, it became a divisive factor in the life of Belmont." When Belmont greeted the beginning of the 1960s, it still had no African American members; nor were they welcome to join. In 1962, Rev. Abel T. Muzorewa, a member of the then–Rhodesia Annual Conference, came to Belmont along with his wife and three sons. By all accounts, they were warmly received by individual Belmonters and the Sunday school class they joined. However, when Mrs. Muzorewa requested that her membership be transferred to Belmont, the then-senior pastor—believing that Belmont was not yet ready to receive a member of color—denied the request, presumably fearing fallout from approximately one-third of the congregation that opposed having a non-white member. For a church supporting missionaries throughout the world, including in Africa, and committed to serving its diverse community, there was a disconnect when it came to membership in the church.

While divisions continued to fester within Belmont, Methodism within America was reuniting. In 1968, The Methodist Church (which had reunited the North and the South in 1938) and The Evangelical United Brethren Church came together to form The United Methodist Church. Many of the denomination's agencies were located in Nashville. And as the Great Society programs of the 1960s embraced greater unity and sought an end to racial discrimination, so too did Belmont United Methodist Church. Conversations and education within Belmont focused on the plight of African Americans, school integration and busing, and other social justice efforts demanding church leadership. By 1977, Belmont was protested not because of its exclusion but because of its inclusion. Protesters picketed around Belmont when it hosted a gathering of the Tennessee Annual Conference, carrying signs attacking The United Methodist Church for being a member of the National Council of Churches. One well-known Belmonter led her own counterprotest, carrying a sign extolling: "Right on: NCC and WCC." And in a fitting gesture of how much Belmont had transformed, Bishop Muzorewa returned in

1977 to preach at Belmont, fifteen years after his wife had been denied membership. By the following year, Belmont became the host for the Nashville Korean Church. Belmont ushered in the new century by welcoming a new fellowship of refugees and immigrants from the Golden Triangle area where Laos, Myanmar, and Thailand meet. This fellowship would grow to be several hundred strong and enrich the multicultural and multiracial nature of Belmont. By embracing diversity, hospitality, and inclusiveness, Belmont retained its vitality as it transitioned from a suburban church into an urban church.

People join a congregation for many reasons. Many participate in a faith community because of need for or support for families. The two of us epitomize those reasons. One of us was baptized in the church and grew up at Belmont. The other came to Belmont when looking for a community of faith in which to raise his children.

Through its preaching and programs, Belmont tends to attract mission- and service-oriented followers who see the role of the congregation as a moral compass and instigator for justice, as articulated and practiced by Jesus Christ. Methodists call this social holiness.

For a church located in the buckle of the Bible Belt of the South, Belmont conversations about same-gender relationships began relatively early. These efforts were led by a ministry team of the church that offered educational and discussion opportunities. Many of these educational and discussion opportunities spilled over in Sunday school classes.

In the spring of 2007, Phil's Sunday school class of twenty- and thirty-year-olds—named the Genesis class—undertook a six-week program on faith, sexual orientation, and The United

Methodist Church. For many, it was the first introduction to the denomination's prohibition on same-gender marriages and, more broadly, *The Book of Discipline.* This programming led to a small-group discussion on what the class could affirm—as a group—in relation to welcoming and supporting persons of all sexual orientations. And assuming that such an affirmation was shared by the entire class, how this could be best expressed in the class description through specific acts of hospitality, outreach, and Christian love. So the class embarked on several weeks of additional education and discernment, which also included deciding whether the class itself would actively stand and work against the denomination's official positions regarding sexual orientation, and whether or not to affiliate with the Reconciling Ministries Network.

Over the next several weeks, the class read a wide array of materials on what the Bible implies about human sexuality (ranging from the late Walter Wink, a theologian and progressive activist at Auburn Theological Seminary, to Richard Hays, a moderate biblical scholar at Duke Divinity School). We met with the local outreach coordinator of the Reconciling Ministries Network, and had one-on-one conversations with every class member, senior church staff, other Sunday school classes, and a former bishop. The process evoked many sincere responses in person and through the class's electronic Listserv that served as a conduit, albeit imperfect, for continued discussion throughout the week. As one member of the class expressed: "I would like to thank all those who have taken leadership roles in [the] class and invited the depth and breadth of discussion which we are afforded every week. While it is at times tasking, the opportunity is nonetheless a tremendous privilege. I personally would otherwise have none of the stimulating debate and challenge to discover and redefine my beliefs with this much knowledge and experience at my disposal...and that is long overdue. I make no promises to rise to the occasion *well*, but am grateful."

In order to gauge more accurately the will and discernment of the Sunday school class, an Internet-based assessment tool was utilized. The reactions expressed that every member of the class (at least of the thirty-three who participated in the exercise) was "in favor of welcoming all persons to our Sunday School Class regardless of sexual orientation." Yet, one in five regarded sexual relationships between persons of the same gender as sinful. However, only two-thirds thought that the class description/ mission statement should reflect the class's openness to persons of all sexual orientations. And less than half (44 percent) were in favor of affiliating with the Reconciling Ministries Network, a proponent of denominational change for marriage equality. And several of those expressed reservations if others in the class disagreed. Yet only four class members (12 percent) said that it would affect their participation in the class if the class made a decision on whether to affiliate different from their own preference. This revelation was significant, suggesting that class members felt more strongly about their relationships with one another than they did with whether the class affiliated with Reconciling Ministries Network.

The discernment provided a wide array of perspectives. Some believed that marriage and ordination were to be decided by the denomination itself and thus were not something with which the class should be concerned. There were also sentiments that the class and Belmont itself were already welcoming. In fact, the comment was made that "we have had several homosexuals in our class over the years and I don't think they have ever felt unwelcome participating in our class." By contrast, another class member expressed that he "learned very early that there were two kinds of people in the world—the people who know how to love unconditionally and the ones who don't." He explained that "the ability to love unconditionally is the truest and most pure gift that God can give. Scriptures provide us insight and guidance in how to handle specific instances in our lives—the bible teaches us how to love. If there is one thing we should add to our mission statement, it's that we are dedicated to learning how to love unconditionally."

For some within a congregation, a Sunday school class or small group is their faith family. These groups of people often form close bonds and become a faith community within the larger church. The diverse views offered by this particular Sunday school class served as a case study for the discussion both within Belmont and the larger denomination. While the discussion within the Sunday school class revealed disagreement and divergent views, it also revealed a common love for one another and their church.

In the same exercise by which class members were asked to express their views and feelings about marriage and ordination of LGBTQ individuals within the church, they were also asked to reflect on what made the Sunday school class special. The feedback reflected genuine appreciation for one another. Appreciation was expressed for the "safe space" to have deep conversations with fellow participants who were the equivalent of an "extended family." Members of the class explained that the Sunday school class was a critical part of their spiritual journey.

While all class members expressed appreciation for the opportunity to learn and be in conversation, there was also concern about decisions being made by smaller groups of people without the involvement of the whole class. And while class members expressed the belief that just having the conversation brought the class closer together, the seeds of fracture were being sown. Some class members lamented that Sunday school topics had become "too heavy" and questioned the willingness of all members to truly listen to one another.

In October of that year, Troy Plummer, executive director of the Reconciling Ministries Network, was in town for a Reconciling Ministries board meeting in Nashville. It was suggested to Rev. Plummer that he spend the Sunday school hour with Phil's Sunday school class. There, Rev. Plummer helped educate class members about RMN and addressed what exactly it meant to affiliate with RMN, including what the ramifications might be for the class, for the clergy in the class, and for the clergy in our church. Although the timing of Rev. Plummer's visit was not intended to necessarily reopen discussion of affiliating with RMN, that is what occurred.

Within nine months, the class split into two. Although the process was facilitated by an outside moderator, it brought up a wealth of emotions among class members. Tears were shed. Feelings were hurt. Promises were made to continue to love one another. To the church as a whole, the split was billed as the birthing of two new classes instead of the destruction of a class. One of the new classes, Portico, would focus on "front porch" ministry. The other class, Kairos, would describe themselves as a "living room" ministry.

Our classes learned an important lesson through this experience. The discussions around sexual orientation focused around ascertaining right from wrong: the "correct" interpretation of biblical scripture, the "correct" understanding of science, the "correct" words to express hospitality, and the "correct" method to articulate church law. In so doing, the sharing of personal stories and the development of deeper relationships took a back seat. In retrospect, the class had engaged on an entirely avoidable path toward division.

Were the conversations around sexual orientation responsible for the split? Yes and no. On one hand, the conversations brought to the surface feelings of uncertainty, distrust, and even exclusion. Sunday school had been a "safe" place, but the nature of the "right and wrong" conversations created tension both between members and within each of us. On the other hand, the nature of the split suggested that the conversations on sexual orientation were more of a proxy than the proximate cause. In other words, the split was not the result of some spiritual divide over sexual orientation. For most every member of the class, sexual orientation and the church's treatment of those in same-gender relationships was not something that they thought about on a regular basis, or even at all outside of conversations during the Sunday school hour.

Instead, the class split almost exactly along the lines of those who had been in the class for six or more years and those who had joined the class more recently. At the end of the day, the two classes that emerged were more about the relationships among members than they were about philosophical or faith differences. Most every group has experienced a similar dynamic, whether it be a faith community, business organization, or even entire civil society. Persons will become more connected with some than others. These connections then lead to the formation of subgroups.

And while these subgroups have more in common with one another than they have differences, too often it is those differences that become the focus. And once in focus, it is difficult for groups of seemingly similar and like-minded persons to refocus on what continues to connect them.

4

THE LEGAL
PROHIBITION

While conversations and efforts were afoot in a Nashville congregation, Tennesseans were having broader political conversations. Earlier, in 1996, the state legislature had enacted a statutory ban on same-gender weddings, captioned "Marriage between one man and one woman only legally recognized marital contract." The law declared that Tennessee's public policy was to recognize the family as "essential to social and economic order and the common good and as the fundamental building block of our society." To promote that policy, the legislature decreed, only a marriage between one man and one woman would be recognized in the state. If another state or foreign jurisdiction were to permit any other type of marriage, "any such marriage shall be void and unenforceable in this state." Tennessee was not alone; every southern state had some variation of these nonrecognition laws. These laws were passed as a reaction to the fact that some states had begun to permit marriages for same-gender couples.

By 2004, however, concern mounted that such a statutory ban could be overturned by the Tennessee Supreme Court based on the state constitution. Accordingly, proponents of the ban sought a state constitutional amendment enshrining the prohibition. The proposed amendment to the state's constitution would define the relationship of one man and one woman as "the only legally recognized marital contract in this state."

To amend the Tennessee constitution, successive state general assemblies must approve the measure, which then must be ratified by a majority of citizens voting for governor, voting in favor of the constitutional amendment. In 2004, the Tennessee House of Representatives approved the ban by a vote of 85 to 5, with the state Senate following suit by a vote of 28 to 1. In 2005, the House and Senate again voted in favor of the proposed amendment, by votes of 88 to 7 and 29 to 3, respectively.

One may take a step back and ask why such a ban was necessary. What interest does a state or civil society have in prohibiting two persons of the same gender from entering into a lifelong commitment to each other? What is the purpose of offering legal rights and obligations to an opposite-gender couple but not a same-gender couple? In other words, what is the state's interest in treating couples differently based on gender? These questions would take on substantial, if not determinative, significance years later in the US Supreme Court. While sociologists and pollsters have measured attitudes toward sexual orientation and same-gender marriage over the years, they have spent less time asking about the origins of those attitudes.

Some studies have suggested that attitudes toward sexual orientation follow attitudes toward the origin of one's sexual orientation. Those who understand sexual orientation to be biological in nature tend to have a more inclusive attitude than those who believe sexual orientation is nonbiological in origin. But that does not answer the ultimate question of why the strong public opinion—at least in the 1990s and early 2000s—in favor of prohibiting same-gender couples from the same marriage rights that the law afforded to opposite-gender couples.

In our work within the church and the legal system, we have thought about this question. For example, does a person who is attracted to someone of the opposite gender feel threatened by someone who is attracted to someone of the same gender? Are heterosexual couples fearful that their marriages would be impaired if marriage was available to all couples regardless of persons' genders? If such fears exist, do they account for the rush to enact legal prohibitions in the 1990s and first decade of the new millennium? In our experience, we do not think so. While we frequently encountered sentiments purporting to defend "traditional" marriage, such explanations were never cast in terms of fear that marriages between opposite-gender persons would somehow be impugned or harmed absent prohibitions on marriage between same-gender persons.

We have also considered whether altruism may be a motivating factor. Could it be that by banning same-gender weddings, people believe that they are somehow helping gay and lesbian persons? We certainly have encountered those who believe that sexual orientation does not arise from biological origins. And we have encountered those who believe that sexual intimacy between those of the same gender was somehow harmful or "wrong"; "harm" certainly appears to have a motivating factor in the prohibitions enacted by The United Methodist Church. But such sentiments suggest a "we know better than you" attitude that does not square with either Christian teachings grounded in love and universal dignity or constitutional constructs grounded in individual freedom and equality. On a more fundamental level, we must ask if wary or paternalistic persons ever tried to fully understand what it means to be gay or lesbian? Have they ever listened to the stories of gay and lesbian persons?

If it is not fear or paternal instinct, then what was the interest that drove these legal prohibitions? "Religion" and "tradition" are frequently given. However, what is it about "religion"? How is one's faith furthered by denying same-gender couples the right to marry? And if we are talking about the Judeo-Christian faith, then are we talking about a handful of Bible verses serving as the entire basis? Given the context of those verses, surely those verses cannot explain the opposition to same-gender marriage, especially when an exponentially larger number of verses could easily be used to justify unequal treatment of the genders and races, including slavery itself. Given Jesus's emphasis on love of all persons, "religion" does not seem to be a justification for discrimination.

As for tradition, what is really meant? The tradition of marriage itself has changed over the years as recounted earlier. Marriage was traditionally between members of the same race. That does not mean it was right to prohibit interracial marriage. And marriage was traditionally between one dominant and one submissive person. That too was unjust. So enacting prohibitions, whether they be civil laws or church strictures, on the basis of tradition really does not explain the underlying motivating factor.

So what was really responsible? Some suggest that the root of opposition to marriage equality, and LGBTQ rights more broadly, is grounded in a pervasive kind of discomfort around human sexuality. Most people we have encountered as church leaders and as legal advocates simply do not want to talk about sex. It is a taboo subject. More than any other sentiment we have encountered, it appears that people have a visceral reaction toward sexual acts different from whatever sexual conduct they find individually appealing. Yet, instead of stating this as basis for their positions, most people use proxies.

This was certainly the case of the debate within the Tennessee legislature. There was absolutely no discussion about sex. Instead, during their consideration of the proposed amendment, the topic of religion and tradition repeatedly crept into the consideration by the Tennessee General Assembly. One legislator, who voted in favor of the amendment, explained during debate on the proposed amendment that "God said it in the beginning, that it was between a man and a woman." Nonetheless, this legislator questioned: "I want to know how in the world are we going to put in the Constitution to stop people from sinning when Jesus Christ hadn't stopped them." And while expressing the belief that "I don't think there is anybody in this room perfect enough in their heart to judge another person for Jesus Christ," this legislator explained that "I am gonna support the legislation simply because it is a political hot footing. . . ."

Other legislators likewise injected religious views into the debate of the General Assembly on the proposed amendment. For example, one legislator declared: "The purpose of marriage since, for thousands of years before the dawn of Christianity has been to ensure that children would have parents and a family unit that would take care of them, and to encourage parents to have certain benefits automatically to support the family." Yet another legislator proclaimed: "I think it is a strong move to support the traditional family, and support the family as intended when God created this world."

While elected representatives do not check their religious views at the statehouse steps, the passage of both the statutory and constitutional bans on same-gender marriages served as an example of the purported religious views of some becoming the civil laws for all. Private interest groups and churches also became involved. One such organization, the Family Action Council of Tennessee, was born from the effort to pass the proposed constitutional amendment. Using same-gender marriage as a springboard to rally political action, the Family Action Council of Tennessee took hold to "continue on beyond the ballot issue to champion a biblical perspective on cultural and policy issues in Tennessee before the state Legislature."

More than 80 percent of Tennesseans voting on the proposed amendment in the fall of 2006 voted in favor of the proposed constitutional amendment. According to the Family Action Council of Tennessee, "What a God-orchestrated success that campaign was! Tennessee's amendment passed by the second-highest margin of all 38 states that eventually passed marriage amendments." It was against this backdrop that the effort at our church began to gather momentum and the seeds would be sown for the legal case that we would take to the US Supreme Court.

5

THE SPIRIT STIRS WITHIN OUR CHURCH

By 2010, one of the most active and growing ministry teams within our church was its Reconciling Ministries Team (which would be subsequently renamed Belmonters for Inclusion). The ministry team recognized that conversation and education was the foundation on which any effective transformation must be built. Organized by passionate leaders, it was a small but dedicated group who wanted to change *The Book of Discipline*, but more importantly wanted to affect the hearts and minds of the congregation and the community at large. The ministry team hosted speakers and screened films for both Belmont members and the public at large. These events largely focused on telling stories; and they garnered publicity through the Tennessee Conference along with local newspaper and radio.

In the spring of 2010, our church had its first Sunday school class, which was aptly named "Kairos" (which in the Bible conveys an opportunity or appointed time for action), officially affiliate with the Reconciling Ministries Network. The class, to which Phil belonged, was one of the two that had originally split. Instead of focusing on scripture and trying to ascertain biblical "truth" about sexual orientation, the class heard and shared stories. Our church's inclusion ministry team had published a booklet of member stories that served as a template. These stories reflect the power of the narrative:

> During high school, one of my best friends was a boy whom I'll here call Jake. We enjoyed playing tennis, going water skiing, playing board games, helping each other with homework, and just hanging out. After high school we went to different colleges, but we kept up with each other and stayed friends.
>
> Jake never did date anyone, and though we saw each other infrequently, I was aware of a depression and sense of loneliness slowly invading his life, especially as his close friends got married and he remained alone.
>
> It was only when Jake committed suicide that I realized that he was gay and unable to reach out to others for support.
>
> It is my strong belief that Jake's inability to accept himself as a gay man could have been changed into a strong sense of self-worth if he had only received the good news of Christ's welcoming acceptance, and of the peace that comes with the message of grace. I pray that our church will change and become a place that ensures that Gay, Lesbian, Bi-sexual and Transgender persons can be supported in authentically embracing themselves as God created them to be.

Such stories and those of class members turned the focus to love for another and away from debating right and wrong.

The class also revisited the prophetic words of Dr. Martin Luther King Jr. in his "Letter from a Birmingham Jail." This modern-day gospel would play a continuing role in our church's journey over the subsequent years and serve as a constant voice in the back of our minds while we put our faith into action within and outside the church. King's words resonated on multiple levels. First, the letter describes the interrelatedness of all communities. As King wrote, injustice anywhere is a threat to justice everywhere. It is not enough for a church community to practice and preach justice within its own walls; instead, it is the duty of every Christian to be an agent for justice anywhere injustice is present. Thus while the general sense both within the Sunday school class and our church itself was one of inclusion, the reality was that LGBTQ persons had long suffered exclusion and the United Methodist denomination itself continued to label them as "incompatible with Christian teaching."

Second, King's letter imparts the importance of urgency. Time is not an agent for change. Instead, people are agents of change and when they are not acting for justice, injustice continues to prevail. King describes the fierce urgency of now and recites the familiar refrain that justice delayed is justice denied. This concept of justice delayed traces back to the time of Jesus and became memorialized in such civil foundational laws as Magna Carta.

Third, King articulates the difference between just laws and unjust laws. His letter that was smuggled out of his jail cell was a response to a group of Alabama clergy who had written an open letter suggesting that King's tactics and mere presence were disturbing their efforts toward convincing their own congregants to follow the law, including Supreme Court precedent striking down desegregation. The letter from the eight clergymen followed an open letter three months earlier, titled "An Appeal for Law and Order and Common Sense," in which they explained:

> It is clear that a series of court decisions will soon bring about desegregation of certain schools and colleges in Alabama. Many

sincere people oppose this change and are deeply troubled by it. As southerners, we understand this. We nevertheless feel that defiance is neither the right answer nor the solution. And we feel that inflammatory and rebellious statements can lead only to violence, discord, confusion, and disgrace for our beloved state.

Having urged their congregants and fellow persons of faith to follow the law, they expressed dismay over King's "unlawful" protests. In response, King wrote that one has both a legal and moral obligation to obey just laws. Conversely, King explains that we have a moral obligation to disobey laws that are unjust. King then distinguishes between just and unjust laws based on whether they comport with the laws of morality as taught by Jesus Christ. Based on this distinction, King explained how he could advise people to follow the Supreme Court's decision in *Brown v. Board of Education* while advocating for people to disobey local laws and ordinances imposing segregation—the former was morally just while the latter was morally bankrupt. King thus explains, using an appeal to Christian "law," how one can advocate breaking some laws while obeying others.

Fourth, King takes issue with separating "the sacred and the secular," expressing his disappointment with fellow Christian ministers dismissing the struggle to rid the country of racial and economic injustice as social issues of which the gospel has no concern. King reminds us of the role of the church in changing unjust civil laws dating back to the refusal of Shadrach, Meshach, and Abednego to obey the laws of Nebuchadnezzar. King explains how early Christians sought to change unjust laws of the Roman Empire even when it meant facing physical punishment and even death. King laments when the church was very powerful, based not on political or economic power, but based instead on its moral leadership in the face of political or societal persecution. Christians would rejoice in their suffering for standing up for morality within civil laws. According to King, the church at that point in time did not merely take the temperature of popular opinion and ideas but instead set the temperature for societal mores. The church, though small in numbers, was big in commitment and by its example and perseverance brought an end to evils such as infanticide and gladiatorial contests. King expresses gratitude toward those "noble souls" who broke from organized religion and its "paralyzing chains of conformity" to join in the fight for justice, freedom, and equality. King acknowledges that some will go to jail and some will be dismissed from their churches or lose the support of their bishops but that they have followed their faith "that right defeated is stronger than evil triumphant."

Fifth, King expresses his disappointment with the majority of his clergy brethren who chose to remain in the security of their sanctuaries, preferring the absence of tension over the fight for equality. King's most indicting criticism explains that the freedom movement's greatest impediment was not the Ku Klux Klan member but the "white moderate" who was concerned more with order than with justice. King predicts that we Christians will have to repent not just for hateful words and action but also for well-meaning people's "appalling silence." According to King, "shallow understanding from people of good will is more frustrating than absolute misunderstanding from people of ill will." And it is at this point that King returns to his warning against the sense of inevitability, explaining that human progress has never rolled in on the wheels of inevitability but instead has come through the unwavering efforts of those willing to work along with God because without such efforts, the forces of inertia prevail.

Finally, King addresses being labeled "an extremist" and explains that he has come to embrace the term. After all, King asks, was not Jesus an extremist himself? King answers his question by quoting scripture: "Love your enemies, bless them that curse you, do good to them that hate you, and pray for them which despitefully use you, and persecute you." King then goes through a list of extremists, transcending both Christian tradition and American civil society, calling out the likes of Amos, Paul, Martin Luther, John Bunyan, Abraham Lincoln, and Thomas Jefferson. King states that the question is not whether Christ followers will be extremists but instead what kind of extremists will they be: extremists for hate or love, for justice or injustice, for equality or inequality. King expresses his frustration with those religious leaders whom he thought would be the strongest allies, but instead failed to speak out and chose only to protect themselves.

The prophetic words of King became the touchstone by which the Kairos Sunday school class viewed its role within a congregation, the denomination, and society when responding to God's call that all persons be recognized and celebrated for their sacred worth. Through the listening of stories of those suffering inequality, including exclusion from ordination and the right to marry, class members felt compelled to act. And King's "Letter from a Birmingham Jail" gave them the framework for action. It would be a framework that would come to guide the rest of Belmont United Methodist Church as well. The Sunday school class decided to affiliate with the Reconciling Ministries Network, holding a worship service to celebrate the occasion, which included the sharing of stories from the congregation of LGBTQ persons and family members, while affirming the Sunday school class's welcoming and celebration of people of all sexual orientations and gender identities in the full life of the church.

6

OUR FAITH-INSPIRED ACTION

While efforts to push for marriage equality were afoot within our church, two important legal cases underway would come to shape our future involvement. In November 2008, Californians passed Proposition 8, which defined marriage as the union of a man and a woman. This voter initiative was quickly challenged in court. On August 4, 2010, a federal trial court in California found that the ban on the marriage of persons of the same gender violated the constitutional due process and equal protection rights of gay and lesbian persons. The federal judge enjoined the enforcement of Proposition 8 but suspended the decision pending appeal. It would be appealed.

An ultimately more significant legal challenge would be filed on November 9, 2010, in New York federal court. This lawsuit was filed by a widow, Edith Windsor, whose same-gender spouse had passed away. When Ms. Windsor's spouse died, the estate was left to Ms. Windsor; under federal estate tax laws assets passing to a surviving spouse are exempt from federal estate taxes. Although New York recognized their marriage, the federal government did not pursuant to the federal Defense of Marriage Act ("DOMA"). Accordingly, Ms. Windsor was denied the same federal tax treatment as surviving spouses of opposite-gender marriages. Ms. Windsor sued over this equal protection violation, and the Obama administration ultimately elected not to defend the lawsuit on the basis that the administration agreed with Windsor's position that the applicable section of DOMA refusing to recognize state marriage law violated the US Constitution. However, the case would be defended by counsel representing Congress.

On June 6, 2012, the New York federal judge ruled that section 3 of DOMA violated Ms. Windsor's due process guarantees under the federal constitution and ordered the federal government to issue the tax refund. This decision was quickly affirmed by the US Court of Appeals for the Second Circuit.

Meanwhile, the challenge to California's Proposition 8 had likewise reached the federal appellate court, with the US Court of Appeals for the Ninth Circuit affirming the district court's injunction based on a 2–1 decision. Proponents of both Proposition 8 and DOMA sought review by the US Supreme Court. On December 7, 2012, the Supreme Court announced that it would hear the pair of cases. While we, like the rest of the nation, were following the cases with some interest, we were also learning what it meant to undertake a high-profile civil rights case. And it all started in Sunday school class at our church.

It was a Sunday morning in July 2008, during the sharing of prayer concerns, that one of Phil's fellow class members sought prayers for a woman named Juana Villegas. Ms. Villegas had just experienced a horrific experience at the hands of Nashville's sheriff's office; the story had been carried in *The New York Times* and had reverberated around Nashville, especially in the immigrant rights community.

Ms. Villegas, a citizen of Mexico, had been driving home from a prenatal appointment. It was likely her last before the expected birth of her fourth child. She and another driver approached a car stopped to make a left turn, and drove around that car in the right lane that was nominally designated for right turns only. Both cars were pulled over by a police officer. The white male in the first car was allowed to leave. Ms. Villegas was not.

Ms. Villegas provided the officer with documentation of Mexican citizenship, but she did not have a US driver's license. The police officer told Ms. Villegas that she would need to call a relative with a US driver's license to drive her vehicle home. Ms. Villegas and her three children would sit in the hot car, on July 3, for more than an hour awaiting the arrival of the relative. When the relative arrived, Ms. Villegas was relieved that she could get her children home. However, the police officer had a different plan. The officer abruptly told Ms. Villegas that she should say goodbye to her children as he placed Ms. Villegas in handcuffs and led her to his squad car.

Nashville was participating in a program called "287(g)" at the time, in which the sheriff's office would work with Immigration and Customs Enforcement ("ICE") to detain persons suspected of being in the country without proper documentation. Perhaps feeling that it was his mission to arrest persons he suspected of lacking the proper documentation to be in the country—for which he apparently earned the nickname "ICE man"—the officer arrested Ms. Villegas and took her to the Nashville jail for processing. Because of the 287(g) program, an "immigration hold" was placed on Ms. Villegas that impeded her ability to post bond.

After being held at the Detention Center for two days—on charges of passing on the right—Ms. Villegas went into labor and her water broke. Ms. Villegas was placed on a gurney with her legs shackled together with leg irons and her wrists handcuffed together. Ms. Villegas remained shackled and handcuffed as she was loaded into an ambulance, driven to Metro General Hospital, unloaded from the ambulance, and taken to a hospital room. One of the transporting officers questioned his supervisor's orders about shackling Ms. Villegas because of the possibility that the baby might arrive on the way to the hospital before he could take off the shackles. He was told to keep Ms. Villegas in the shackles.

At the hospital, Ms. Villegas was lifted—while still shackled and handcuffed—from the stretcher onto the hospital bed. The attending doctor found Ms. Villegas in "severe pain with contractions." Ms. Villegas would then be shackled to the hospital bed and would remain shackled for the next hour while in labor, even though she was having contractions every two minutes of fifty- to sixty-second durations.

Thankfully, shortly before Ms. Villegas gave birth, an officer assigned to "guard" her decided to disregard policy and unshackle Ms. Villegas. However, after Ms. Villegas gave birth, the shackles were reapplied. Ms. Villegas remained chained to her bed for the duration of her two-day postpartum recovery, including the time she slept, held her newborn son, and nursed him. Even when using the bathroom or taking a shower, Metro's officers shackled Ms. Villegas's legs together. And throughout this time period, Ms. Villegas was prohibited from speaking to or seeing her husband or family.

When Ms. Villegas was discharged after two days of postpartum recovery in shackles, she was provided a breast pump because she was being separated from her newborn. The sheriff's office refused to allow Ms. Villegas to take the breast pump back to the jail despite pleas from the medical staff. Once at the jail, Ms. Villegas was unable to express her milk without the breast pump, her breasts became engorged, and she developed mastitis. Ms. Villegas's breasts became "rock hard" and she experienced excruciating pain. Ms. Villegas was rendered unable to move and resorted to asking another inmate to try futilely to express Ms. Villegas's milk.

While only a few of these details would be originally reported, enough details had emerged that we felt compelled to act. We had never tried, much less brought, a civil rights action of this significance. Yet, after hearing the plight of Ms. Villegas, we felt compelled by our faith to act. And so we did.

The next eight months would be a whirlwind of action as we, along with our law partner John Farringer, received a crash course in civil rights litigation. We were fortunate to have more experienced lawyers from both local and national rights organizations willing to teach us and we worked with an excellent immigration attorney, Elliott Ozment, who had found his calling serving the underserved immigrant population of Nashville. Together, we would bring a lawsuit on behalf of Ms. Villegas against the Metropolitan Government of Nashville, whose policies had required that Ms. Villegas be shackled while in labor. The goal was not money damages, even though Ms. Villegas had suffered both physically and emotionally. Instead, the goal was to ensure that this would not happen to anyone again. Women in labor should not be shackled during labor. And local police should not arrest persons based solely on the color of their skin or language they speak.

The case would attract significant local media attention and with it, our first taste of backlash because of our advocacy. The comments left on local media sites were not kind. They included comments such as the following:

- ACORN! They instigated this whole thing, that I am sure! When they registered her to vote they probably planted the seed to sue the sheriff! If the Founding Fathers could come back today, they would kick that lawyer who represented her in the nuts!

- I propose as a form of protest by American Citizens to not ever do business with her attorney. Make it so hard for him to earn a living; he has to leave Middle, TN!

- Are you kidding me? Sure, 90% for these despicable attorneys and the rest for this illegal alien who (1) violated US law, (2) drove without a license, (3) exploited the generosity of the American people, and the list goes on.

- This woman is a parasite. . . .

- Let me get this straight. . . . The woman was here illegally, driving without a license, most likely uninsured, and breaking the law, but she is rewarded . . . ? As far as I am concerned, her rights ended whenever she broke the laws of our land by entering and living here illegally. The "do-gooders" who continue to enable this kind of behavior are a big part of the reason this country is in the current financial mess it's in right now. . . .

Nevertheless, we persisted with the case. And for good reason: Juana Villegas. We quickly discovered that we gained far more from representing Juana than we could ever contribute. She was both an inspiration to us and a reminder of why we went to law school. She also confirmed our faith. While we were able to use our privilege of position to advance her case, it became a personal privilege to get to know Juana and her family. She was truly dedicated to making the world better for others, even at her own expense. And this was never more on display than in the goals that she wanted to achieve with the lawsuit.

We had been able to secure a stay of deportation for Juana so long as the litigation lasted. A resolution of the lawsuit would therefore mean her imminent separation from her children (who were all US citizens) and the only country she had known for the past twenty years. It would have been easy, and completely understandable, for Juana to resist any resolution or demand money damages commensurate with the physical and psychological harm she experienced. Instead, Juana was willing to settle the case for *zero* dollars in exchange for the Nashville government entering into a court order whereby it would refrain from shackling women in labor (absent some specific threat such as flight risk or violence) and stop detaining suspected immigration law violators whose only charges are nonviolent traffic violations.

It is an image still vividly burned into our brains as we explained to Juana that resolving the case on such a basis would mean her immediate deportation and separation from her husband and children. With tears trickling down her face, Juana looked at both of us and simply said, in broken English, that she did not want anyone else to suffer what she had to suffer. For Juana, that was the entire reason for bringing the lawsuit and if she could accomplish that, she would continue to suffer for the greater good.

The moment was unlike anything we had ever experienced in the practice of law, and in that moment, it became apparent that while we helped give Juana a voice, it was Juana who was the true hero. The city of Nashville never agreed to Juana's simple request, and the case did not settle. And having been witness to Juana's ultimate act of selflessness, we felt all the more responsibility to represent Juana to the fullest extent of our abilities. We ended up taking Juana's case to a federal jury trial.

Not only did Juana's case represent our most significant civil rights case, but for Phil it was also his first jury trial. The case had become all-consuming, and for a trio of business litigators, a departure from what was comfortable and familiar. We needed expert medical witnesses, who could both testify as to the medical harm posed by shackling and the deep psychological harm inflicted by her treatment. Our extended faith family helped fill that need. Dr. Sandra Torrente, who was a friend of a fellow Sunday school class member, volunteered to serve as an expert witness. Dr. Torrente worked at the very hospital where Juana gave birth and testified as to the medical dangers posed by shackling.

Dr. Jill DeBona was the parent of a friend of Phil's kindergarten-age daughter and she had grown up with a bilingual father who was a professor of Spanish. It felt like a "God-thing." Dr. DeBona could both speak with Juana in her native language while being able to relate her medical findings in English to the jury. As a clinical psychiatrist, Dr. DeBona conducted numerous hours of psychiatric interviews with Ms. Villegas along with her family, friends, and employer. She diagnosed Juana as suffering from PTSD; after all, during labor, she could not move or open her legs. Unable to move or open her legs, she feared that her son would not be able to be delivered. Juana had to sit with the terror that her baby might die inside of her body.

At trial, Ms. Villegas testified: "I feared for my child… if he were to come while I was there in the ambulance, I didn't know if I was going to be able to open my legs so that he could come out." This fear would haunt Juana in the years that followed, as she described the shackling as "always" on her mind because she has memories "when I see my son," especially on his birthday. As Dr. DeBona testified:

> Ms. Villegas experienced thirty-six hours of shackling with a heavy leg iron. This shackling was degrading and humiliating. Ms. Villegas's self concept is that she is a mother, a worker, a wife, not a criminal. This humiliation at the hands of the police has caused a break in trust, in the institutions and people that are supposed to protect her. Her core sense of self, as a human being with value, has been shaken. Her sense of security has been shattered. A traffic violation can lead to thirty-six hours of shackling.

Phil gave the closing argument. It was the first time he had given a closing argument to a jury. The jury then returned a verdict, awarding Juana $200,000 in damages. The hug that Juana gave us when the jury announced its verdict was the best and most memorable gift we had ever received from a client. Moreover, the jury verdict paved the way for Ms. Villegas and her husband to receive U Visas, allowing them to remain in the United States on an eventual path toward permanent residency.

Throughout our representation, our faith fueled us and our faith community supported us. Our extended church family would offer assistance and support throughout our journey. Indeed, when our retiring senior pastor, Ken Edwards, would give his final sermon many years later, he would lift up Juana Villegas and our collective advocacy on her behalf as the exemplar of how our church puts faith in action.

However, our representation of Ms. Villegas did not end with the jury verdict. The Nashville government appealed the decision to the US Court of Appeals for the Sixth Circuit. Two of the three judges on the panel were openly hostile to our position during the oral argument. It was a tough day for us. It would not be the last time that this appellate court would challenge us in a civil rights case. As we traveled back from Cincinnati, where the appellate court is located, we discussed what would be next. Our appetite and appreciation for civil rights litigation had only grown as a result of representing Juana. Our conversation turned toward marriage equality, and we strategized for the next few hours. We were not sure how to become involved or whether such an opportunity would ever be possible. But our faith compelled us to act, and we had learned that acting had brought us faith.

Our faith would prepare us for what would happen next. Several months after the argument in the Sixth Circuit, we received a divided opinion from the Court overturning the jury verdict based on a pretrial procedural deficiency, at least according to two of the judges. The case was not over, but we would need to retry the case. Our immediate thought concerned subjecting Juana and her family to another emotionally vexing trial, where Juana would be forced to relive her trauma again. So we geared up to try the case again. A new legal director had assumed the role as Nashville's top legal counsel, and he readily recognized the detriment to the city of going through another public trial. Our faith then intervened.

We decided to break bread over dinner with counsel for the city. Phil even shared a whole fish entrée with the legal director. During this dinner, we spoke frankly and freely about resolving the case. The city agreed. They would compensate Juana for her damages and the city had stopped both shackling and its participation in the 287(g) program. It was exactly as Juana had wanted: what happened to her would not happen to anyone else. And the effects went well beyond Nashville. The case had the effect of changing the shackling policy of women in labor throughout the country.

Today, Juana still has some residual symptoms of the trauma. However, she has also become a voice for the immigrant community and remains an advocate for social change. The experience of representing Juana had a profound effect on us. It would reinforce our faith and call us to incorporate that faith into our profession. It would show us the power of the narrative and our responsibility to give voice to those who cannot tell their story. It would expand our practice of law and our desire for taking on future civil rights cases. And it would prepare us for our next case.

Chapter 6

7

A FAITH-BASED NARRATIVE FOR MARRIAGE EQUALITY

With the calendars turning to 2012, our church and the broader United Methodist denomination greatly anticipated the General Conference, which occurs every four years. Would this be the year that the exclusionary language of *The Book of Discipline* would change? We were chosen for various leadership roles within our church. Bill would be appointed to the board of trustees while Phil was tapped to become chair of the administrative board, which involved a six-year commitment serving two years each as vice chair, chair, and past chair. These roles bestowed tremendous responsibility but afforded great opportunity to live out our faith within the church as we had learned to do in our professions.

The inclusion ministry team of our church was filled with great passion and energy. It had become one of the most active ministries within the church and felt it was time for our church as a whole to heed the words of Martin Luther King Jr. The inclusion ministry team presented the church leadership with a plan for adoption of a formal proclamation of faith, while also affiliating with the Reconciling Ministries Network. Not everyone within the church leadership was receptive. Some asked why. Our church was already an inclusive place. Why did we need to formally proclaim it? And why would the church need to affiliate with others through the Reconciling Ministries Network? Wasn't it enough that our church did the right thing? Plus, what was the urgency?

King's "Letter from a Birmingham Jail" would play a role in reminding everyone of the importance of action by people of faith. Yet, it was important to recognize that everyone involved was a well-intentioned Christ follower. Those concerned about "rocking the boat" were just as concerned about our church as those wanting to overturn tables. And there was a sincere desire to avoid making existing church members feel alienated from their own congregation and retain the fabric of what made us Christ followers. A welcoming statement was suggested as one way to agree to disagree but nonetheless unite to show hospitality and love to all brothers and sisters. Of course, it was observed by all involved that following Christ is not all about those who are members of a congregation. King's lament about the "white moderate" was invoked to remind everyone of the fierce urgency of acting in the present.

However, as eloquently and prophetically as King spoke of the need for action, it was actually the narratives of participants in the congregation that helped the congregation come together. On May 20, 2012, our church's administrative board met. Nearly one hundred participants, some board members, some there to show support, turned out. It would be a meeting unlike any other.

During the time reserved at each board meeting for the "ministry movement," Phil introduced three long-time church members to speak about the church's inclusion team and the plan for a church-wide discernment. The first, Hugh Wright, had spent his life at the church and was tasked with giving context for the efforts by the inclusion team over the preceding eight months leading up to this point. While this context was important, something magical happened when Hugh shared his own personal witness. Nearly eighty years old, Hugh described the events and his role in them during the 1950s and 1960s when African Americans had been excluded from church membership. He broke down explaining that he had vowed never again to see the church used as an agent of exclusion. As a standard-bearer within the congregation, Hugh's words touched everyone present.

Next, Frank Moore shared his story as a gay church member. His partner of several years, Doug Hagler, also a member and former ordained minister in The United Methodist Church before having to relinquish his credentials because of his sexual orientation, undertook a vigil in the sanctuary before and during Frank's address to the board, praying for him and the church that he loved. Frank was well known in the congregation, having raised his children in the church, sung in the choir, and taken an active role in helping lead the youth group. Not everyone within the church or even those present at the board meeting knew Frank's sexual orientation.

Frank spoke from the heart. He spoke of the importance of Belmont to him, his partner, and their children, all of whom called the church home. With tears flowing down his face, Frank expressed his love for everyone at our church but grieved for his partner having to surrender his credentials, and the countless other LGBTQ persons who had not been welcomed into the full life of The United Methodist Church. Frank expressed his profound sorrow over being unable to unite in Christian marriage with his long-time partner and co-parent their children. Frank was not the only one who became emotional while he spoke. Tears flowed among those in attendance. When Frank finished, every member of the board stood and gave him a standing ovation and spontaneous hugs of love and support.

The final narrative was provided by Jim Strickland, who had previously been on the ministry staff and now, along with his wife, led the older adult ministry team. Jim shared about his own daughter, who had discovered from an early age her call to ministry. However, she had been forced to leave The United Methodist Church because of her sexual orientation, although later, after obtaining a masters of theological studies and serving at an Episcopal church, she was invited to join the staff of a United Methodist Church in a southern state as director of youth ministry. The senior pastor, however, fired her after learning of her sexual orientation. Jim shared his prayer that one day his daughter would be invited back into The United Methodist Church where she had grown up. Jim then outlined plans for a church-wide discernment process on adopting a formal welcoming statement and deciding whether to affiliate with the Reconciling Ministries Network.

Phil ended the presentation with a summary of the tasks ahead for the board and a call for its leadership in the church in the coming months. And although he had prepared a document to answer questions about "why now," "why have a statement when we are already welcoming," "why single out one group in our statement," "why rock the boat on this divisive matter within our congregation," "will we lose members," and "what will be the economic effect," the reality was that the narratives had answered all of those questions. The board was urged to reflect upon the stories and stay following the meeting for the first of several listening sessions, in which the larger group broke out into smaller groups of eight to ten participants. During this session, and those that would follow, a facilitator would engage in active, loving listening techniques while a recorder would capture the thoughts and questions expressed to become part of the discernment process. The purpose was not to debate or discuss but rather to hear one another's narratives and ensure that all voices were heard. The board meeting was followed up by a congregation-wide mailing that included both the narratives and factual information, while asking everyone to participate in the forthcoming listening sessions.

As the listening effort was underway, it became apparent to Belmont's leadership that questions such as the ones our church had in its support for marriage equality brought deeper questions about our identity as a faith community. The listening sessions that had begun by focusing on LGBTQ equality within our church became a platform for understanding who we were as a faith community. Our church therefore utilized the listening session framework to address the broader question of discerning God's will and calling for us as a congregation. The discernment process was intentionally grounded in reflection on scripture and prayer and asked, What are our prayers for our church? What does our church do best? Where is it less successful in building up the kingdom of God? What are the most pressing needs that God is calling us to address together? What is holding us back from fulfilling God's promise? A year-long effort ensued.

During this time, twenty-two listening sessions were held in which more than 250 church members participated. After information was gathered and assimilated from these sessions, four open-forum sessions to refine and develop the strategies stemming from the listening sessions were held that involved 180 church members. Several "validation" sessions were then held to confirm the focus areas, strategies, and tactics that had emerged. The result was a comprehensive strategic plan in which the church confirmed its calling to focus the collective efforts of the congregation in four areas: hospitality, nurturing, diversity, and mission.

The vision cast for each of these areas included:

- **Hospitality:** Living into God's call for hospitality, we will be a church that shows genuine and radical hospitality to all. We accomplish this by professing that as a community of faith, we proclaim God's unconditional love for the world. We believe every person is of sacred worth and created in God's image. We commit to Jesus' example of inclusive love, care, and intentional hospitality with persons of every race, ethnicity, age, sexual orientation, gender identity, marital status, faith story, physical or mental ability, economic status, or political perspective. We respect our diversity of opinion and expressions of faith. Therefore, as God loves us, so let us love and serve in the name of Christ.

- **Nurturing:** Every member of our faith family is engaged in activities and relationships that address spiritual and human needs and offer opportunities for rest, rejuvenation, healing, and growth.

- **Diversity:** Drawing upon the richness of diversity both within and around the congregation, Belmont's vision is to live into God's call, in which we are a church where every person who is a part of the Belmont faith family identifies and understands their gifts and uses them in a constructive way to bring heaven on earth.

- **Mission:** All members of our community of faith undertake mission as a lifestyle using their unique gifts. Our mission activities build relationships, create opportunity, extend justice, and afford respect to those with whom we are in mission.

As the congregation considered these areas, it became clear that the four visions represented not only a singular goal of perfecting discipleship but also a way of life beyond a ministry focus. Thus the vision, strategies, and tactics in the strategic plan were guided by the idea that the church will grow in its faith to the extent that all members engage more deeply in these four areas on a daily basis in their personal and professional lives.

After this lengthy discernment and listening, the board voted to approve the strategic plan and a faith statement about hospitality to all. The minutes from that meeting explain that the faith statement "was not forecasting what [the church] would become, [but] instead described where we are now" in our mission "to bring God to a hurting world." In adopting the statement, the congregation proclaimed that we would "explicitly share our welcome with all persons of all ages and walks of life who enter our doors (either physically or virtually by participating in one of our ministries) through all means possible." Moreover, we would be "explicit [in] welcoming... lesbian, gay, bisexual, and transgender (LGBT) persons and employ tactics to live into this welcoming and make it as effective as possible."

What had begun as an effort to listen to and hear one another on LGBTQ inclusion ended with a coming together of the entire church around our shared expectations. By listening to one another and focusing on one another's basic dignity and sacred worth, we were able to address division and discord through love and a common calling. This was most exemplified in the faith statement that emerged:

> We believe every person is of sacred worth and created in God's image. We commit to Jesus' example of inclusive love, care, and intentional hospitality with persons of every race, ethnicity, age, sexual orientation, gender identity, marital status, faith story, physical or mental ability, economic status, or political perspective. We respect our diversity of opinion and expressions of faith. Therefore, as God loves us, so let us love and serve in the name of Christ.

This faith statement was not an explicit endorsement of marriage equality. In fact, the group that authored the statement and many within the church that supported it included those who, like a majority of Tennesseans at the time, did not endorse same-gender weddings. However, the group—which included a high level of diversity of thoughts and opinions—found common ground in writing a beautiful faith statement that had the powerful effect of affirming the basic dignity and sacred worth of all people, regardless of sexual orientation, a necessary and critical component of any step toward marriage equality within the church or society. And it would change the discourse within our church around the subject of marriage equality, as the focus would become the sacred worth and dignity of each child of God.

8

THE LEGAL CASE FOR MARRIAGE EQUALITY IN TENNESSEE BEGINS

A s our church was discerning God's call for inclusion, our law firm received a different kind of call—an actual phone call. In the summer of 2013, Bill's son, Jay, was a law student at the University of Tennessee. Jay's girlfriend (now wife) Jesse Ford was a fellow law student, and had formed a close friendship with a member of the adjunct faculty named Regina Lambert.

It was late June, and Regina had just read the majority opinion of the US Supreme Court in the case of *Windsor v. United States*, written by Justice Anthony Kennedy. *Windsor* was a huge achievement for the advancement of marriage equality and LGBTQ rights in general. This was the most recent in a string of decisions announcing, in effect, that government had no good reason to discriminate against gay or lesbian citizens. As recently as 1986, in *Bowers v. Hardwick*, the Court had held that the Constitution permitted the state of Texas to criminalize acts of consensual sex between adults of the same gender. That case was overruled in 2003, in *Lawrence v. Texas*, in an opinion also authored by Justice Kennedy that declared that *Bowers* had been wrongly decided.

Regina was thrilled beyond measure with the decision in *Windsor*. She was determined to take things further. Tennessee and many other states had on their books various laws that forbade same-sex marriage and refused recognition to the marriages of same-gender couples, even when they were married in states that expressly authorized those marriages. Regina reached out to Abby Rubenfeld of Nashville and to Maureen Holland of Memphis, both prominent lawyers and gay rights activists. Abby and Maureen were already, independently, ready to act.

Regina set up a conference call with Abby and Maureen, and because of her friendship with Jay and Jesse she invited them to her home to listen to the call. She knew that they would be keenly interested in the ideas that would be discussed. And the main idea was to have a lawsuit in Tennessee to challenge the validity of Tennessee's nonrecognition laws, particularly in light of the *Windsor* decision.

Regina, Abby, and Maureen are each solo practitioners, and they wanted to add a law firm to help bring a case in Tennessee. They had already recruited the National Center for Lesbian Rights (hereafter NCLR) to be part of the team. Some lawyers at large law firms had expressed interest, but the firms had decided not to participate. On the conference call, the discussion centered on how to find a law firm with appropriate resources, inclination, and experience to bring on board.

While listening to the conversation, Jay spoke up and said, "My dad will do it." This was the filial beginning of a two-year journey through the federal court system. Jay called his father from the next room during the conference call, and told him of the discussion. Then Bill got another call from Abby, who then called Phil. Our law firm, Sherrard & Roe, PLC, immediately agreed to become part of the team, and our fellow law partners Scott Hickman and John Farringer joined us on the case. We had worked with John on the Villegas case (see chapter 6), and Scott was eager to become involved. Scott had been a minister prior to entering the legal profession, and he viewed his involvement in the case, like the rest of us, as an expression of his faith.

Abby, Regina, and Maureen had concluded, rightly, that the only way to change the status quo in Tennessee was through a federal lawsuit to declare the nonrecognition laws unconstitutional. It would not happen through a popular vote or legislative act at any time in the foreseeable future. After *Windsor,* many lawsuits to challenge nonrecognition laws were filed around the United States. In some of those cases, plaintiffs asked the courts to require a state to issue them a marriage license and permit them to get married. These types of cases were called "right to marry" cases. In other cases, plaintiffs who were already legally married in a state that recognized same-gender marriages, such as Massachusetts or New York, asked the courts to require another state to recognize the validity of their marriages. These cases were called "recognition" cases.

Windsor had decided that the *federal* government could not deny recognition to a same-gender marriage that was valid in the state where it was contracted. It had expressly not decided whether a *state* government could refuse such recognition. Those who advocated for the preservation of nonrecognition laws found much in Justice Kennedy's opinion to give hope to the argument that federalism principles permitted states to have differing laws on marriage. In fact, the opinion pointed out that the definition of marriage had historically been left up to states, and those laws differed around the country.

The legal team's first decision was to determine what type of case to bring in Tennessee. The NCLR team, headed by Shannon Minter, David Codell, and Chris Stoll, were of the opinion that a recognition case would be the most strategic and expeditious way to chip away at Tennessee's statutory and constitutional bans on same-gender marriage. The rest of the team agreed. It would be an incremental step to expand the holding of *Windsor* to Tennessee. The initial task was to find same-gender married couples who lived in Tennessee and wanted to be plaintiffs in such a case.

As an initial matter, it was obvious to the legal team that any couples willing to become plaintiffs in a civil rights lawsuit asking a court to force Tennessee to recognize same-gender marriages would be in for a potentially long and difficult path. Abby Rubenfeld was a long-time champion for those types of clients. For over thirty-five years she had fought for the rights of gay and lesbian clients in all types of cases. Regina Lambert and Maureen Holland were similarly well known. The three of them were in the best position to find the right plaintiffs. With Abby in Nashville, Regina in Knoxville, and Maureen in Memphis, we had the state pretty well covered.

Perhaps not coincidentally, our law firm had another tie to Abby Rubenfeld that we all came to celebrate together. One of our law partners, Webb Campbell, is the son of the well-known civil rights advocate Will Campbell. Webb's sister, Penny, had been Abby's client in an important case that invalidated Tennessee's sodomy laws. The historical ties among the lawyers would help to unify a legal team that we came to consider a "dream team." We now needed clients.

Choosing plaintiffs was a crucial step. We were looking for couples who had been married in a state that recognized the validity of their marriages, but who now resided in Tennessee. For such couples, their marriages were valid in one state, but "void" in Tennessee. Abby, Regina, and Maureen had heard from many couples who wanted to be part of a suit, and the couples who finally chose to become involved, with their advice and counsel, were ideal. One could not have asked for better plaintiffs or more compelling stories.

Valeria and Sophy

Drs. Valeria Tanco and Sophy Jesty first met by chance in an elevator in September 2009, while they were graduate students in the College of Veterinary Medicine at Cornell University in Ithaca, New York. They started dating in 2010, and had been in love and committed to each other ever since. Valeria and Sophy married in the state of New York on September 9, 2011.

After Sophy completed her postgraduate fellowship in cardiac regenerative medicine at Cornell, they decided to look for jobs that were geographically close to each other so that they could live together, a difficult proposition for two aspiring university-level teachers. The University of Tennessee's College of Veterinary Medicine in Knoxville offered them that opportunity, and they accepted it readily. Sophy became an assistant professor in the Department of Small Animal Clinical Sciences, and Valeria was hired as a clinical assistant professor in Small Animal Reproductive Medicine.

In June 2012, Valeria and Sophy, like so many other married couples, decided to have a child together, and began trying to conceive a child through assisted reproduction. On July 10, 2013, they were thrilled to learn that Valeria was pregnant with their first child, who was due to be born in spring 2014. Under the laws of Tennessee, opposite-gender married couples who conceived a child using alternative insemination were able to take advantage of the statutory presumption that both spouses are the parents of a child born during a marriage. However, because the state of Tennessee did not recognize Valeria and Sophy's marriage, Sophy could not benefit from that marital presumption. In other words, Sophy would lack legal recognition as a parent of her own child—a status that automatically would be granted to any opposite-gender spouse immediately upon the child's birth.

In preparation for the birth of their child, Valeria and Sophy also sought to enroll themselves in a family plan through the health insurance plans of their employer, the University of Tennessee. However, such coverage was denied under the state-sponsored health plan because it defined a spouse as: "Your spouse (legally married)—Article VI, section 18 of the Tennessee Constitution provides that a marriage from another state that does not constitute the marriage of one man and one woman is 'void and unenforceable in this state.'"

Valeria Tanco, Bill Harbison, Regina Lambert, Sophy Jesty

Ijpe and Thom

Sergeant First Class Ijpe DeKoe and Thom Kostura met at camp when they were both teenagers, maintaining a close friendship for over a decade until March 2011, when they decided to start dating as adults. At the time, Ijpe was living in Memphis, Tennessee, and Thom in East Hampton, New York. In late summer 2011, Ijpe, a full-time reservist with the Army Reserves, received orders to deploy to Afghanistan. Before Ijpe's departure, Ijpe and Thom married in New York on August 4, 2011. A week later, Ijpe touched down in Afghanistan to start his nearly yearlong deployment.

Ijpe returned from Afghanistan in May 2012 and moved with Thom to Memphis. From the day they arrived in Tennessee, their relationship enjoyed none of the benefits automatically given to married couples, despite their having been legally married in New York. According to the state of Tennessee and the federal government, their relationship did not exist. For their first year in Memphis, Ijpe continued to work for the US Army Reserves in Memphis. During that time Thom worked while he applied to the master of fine arts program at the Memphis College of Fine Arts. Thom was accepted into the program and started classes in August 2013.

On September 3, 2013, the US Department of Defense began respecting Ijpe and Thom's marriage, consistent with the Supreme Court's ruling in *Windsor v. United States.* As a result, Thom was covered by Ijpe's health insurance, permitted to enter the base, and allowed to access the many services offered to the spouses of members of the military. Although the military fully respected

Ijpe and Thom's marriage, the state of Tennessee treated their marriage as a legal nullity the moment they stepped off the base.

Like other legally married couples, Ijpe and Thom wanted the assurance of knowing that their marriage would be respected by state officials and third parties, and that they would be treated equally under the law to other married couples. The daily injury and stigma of being treated unequally and having their legal marriage treated as a nullity in their home state was particularly painful for Ijpe, who has dedicated his life to protecting the very values of liberty and equal protection that Tennessee denied him, Thom, and their family.

Matthew and Johno

When we met Johno Espejo and Matthew Mansell ("Johno and Matt"), they had been in a committed relationship for more than eighteen years. They had been legally married on August 5, 2008, while they were living in California. Several years before Johno and Matt married, while still living in California, they decided to start a family together by adopting children from the foster care system in Alameda County, California. In December 2007, the county foster care agency placed their oldest child, a boy, in their home when the child was thirteen months old. Approximately five months later, the agency placed a newborn girl in their home. The children quickly became part of the family and were adopted by Johno and Matt on September 25, 2009. Both Johno and Matt are the legal parents of each child. Johno quit his job as a forklift driver to take care of the children, and Matt continued to work.

Matt then began working at a large international law firm in San Francisco conducting administrative services. In 2012, the firm announced that it was planning to centralize all of its administrative services in a new office located in Nashville, Tennessee. Johno and Matt decided to move their family to the Nashville area so that Matt could continue working for his employer.

Matt's employer had instituted policies that sought to offset, to the extent possible under existing law, some of the harms caused by the state of Tennessee's refusal to recognize Johno and Matt as a married couple. But those policies were not sufficient to shield Johno and Matt from many of the harms caused by Tennessee law. Johno, Matt, and their children were denied the equal dignity and respect that comes from legal recognition of their marriage by the state. Every day that Tennessee refused to respect their marriage was a day that their family had to suffer the indignity, stress, and stigma of not knowing whether or when their marriage would be recognized.

These three married couples agreed to become plaintiffs to challenge Tennessee's nonrecognition laws. On a Sunday afternoon in July 2013, Abby arranged a meeting at her office for the clients and lawyers to get to know one another. Ijpe and Thom were not able to come, but the other clients attended. Abby, Maureen, and Regina were there, and Shannon Minter from NCLR. Bill attended as a representative for our firm.

Each person took turns saying who they were, and why they were there. There was not yet any lawsuit prepared, but the common ground of the meeting was to find a way for the courts to declare that the marriages of the three plaintiff couples must be recognized as valid by the state of Tennessee. Everyone knew that the case would draw a great deal of attention, much of it negative.

Chapter 8

The clients and lawyers agreed that everyone was ready to go forward.

Shannon Minter, Sophy Jesty, Chris Stoll, Valeria Tanco, Matthew Mansell, David Codell, Johno Espejo, Abby Rubenfeld, Regina Lambert, Scott Hickman, Maureen Holland, Ijpe Dekoe, John Farringer, Thom Kostura, Phil Cramer, Bill Harbison

9

VICTORY
FOLLOWED BY
DISAPPOINTMENT

With clients on board, our team of lawyers now had to decide how to prepare and file the case. Phil and John listened to hours of legislative debate from the Tennessee archives to understand what the state legislators had discussed in passing the 1996 and 2006 laws restricting marriage to one man and one woman. Virtually all of that discussion was focused on religious reasons for restricting marriage between persons of the same gender.

Scott and Bill researched the ways in which state laws benefited married couples. The list grew overwhelmingly long. Married people are presumed to have authority to act for their spouses if one is disabled or hospitalized; they receive favorable state income tax treatment; they are allowed to own property as "tenants by the entireties," available only to married couples; they have the right to bring a wrongful death suit if one spouse is killed. And there are literally hundreds of other ways in which Tennessee law favors married couples.

To help shore up the fact that these plaintiff couples had the legal standing to sue, the team came up with ideas for them to request things from the state that are available only to married couples. For Val and Sophy, who owned a home, our team prepared a deed titling their property as tenants by the entireties. The register of deeds for Knox County recorded the document, but mailed it back with a letter reminding them that Tennessee did not recognize their marriage and advising that the deed was a nullity.

The legal challenge to Tennessee's nonrecognition laws centered on two basic constitutional doctrines, both found in the Fourteenth Amendment to the US Constitution. The first argument was that marriage is a fundamental right, and a state could not deprive a citizen of a fundamental right without due process of law; the state must demonstrate that there is some compelling state interest to justify the state's action. Here, the state was refusing to recognize marriages of these plaintiffs, and, the team argued, there was no good reason (much less a compelling reason) for the state to do so.

The second argument was based on the equal protection clause of the Fourteenth Amendment. Simply put, the state could not treat persons similarly situated differently without a good reason for doing so. For example, in *Loving v. Virginia*, decided in 1967, the Supreme Court had held that Virginia's laws prohibiting interracial marriage were unconstitutional because they discriminated against persons based solely on race. Here, the state freely recognized marriages of opposite-gender couples, but refused to recognize marriages of same-gender couples.

Part of the framework of marriage laws in the United States has been, for centuries, the "place of celebration" rule. The reasoning of virtually all courts in all states has been that if a marriage is validly contracted in the state where the marriage takes place, the marriage will be recognized as valid by other states. So, for example, although Tennessee does not permit common-law marriages (a legally recognized marriage between two people who did not buy a marriage license or participate together in a ceremony), it will recognize a common-law marriage that was validly contracted in a state that does permit those kinds of marriages.

Finally, a number of Supreme Court precedents hold that citizens have a right to travel feely among the various states. This is a protected "due process" right, so it is related to the first due process clause argument. The three plaintiff couples in this case had all been validly married, but when they traveled to Tennessee their marriages were treated as nullities. The same would be true as they traveled from state to state, some states recognizing the marriages, and some not. The marriages cycled on and off depending on what state they happened to be in at the time. For Thom and Ijpe, the ironies were even more dramatic; they were married when they were on the US army base (because of *Windsor*), but were not treated as married once they stepped off the base in Tennessee. Tennessee's nonrecognition laws, we argued, put an undue burden on the plaintiffs' right to travel. The right-to-travel argument capped off the legal theories for the plaintiffs.

A lawsuit is begun by filing a complaint with an appropriate court. Our legal team chose to file in the US District Court for the Middle District of Tennessee in Nashville. The plaintiffs were from each of the three grand divisions of Tennessee, and Nashville is the state capital. The defendants would be Tennessee's governor, William Edward "Bill" Haslam, and other state officials charged with enforcing the nonrecognition laws. The relief requested in the complaint was a declaration by the Court that these laws were unconstitutional, and that an injunction be issued preventing the state from enforcing the laws.

On the morning of Monday, October 21, 2013, all of the lawyers and most of the clients met at our offices in Nashville to sign the complaint. NCLR had coordinated a press conference. Even though the complaint was being filed in the US District Court, the press conference would be on the steps of the Davidson County Courthouse because that was a good place to invite television film crews.

We walked together to the court square in Nashville. Abby took the lead in explaining the lawsuit to the media, and Bill was interviewed as well. It wasn't complicated, we told the reporters. All of the plaintiffs were lawfully married couples, and the state of Tennessee was refusing to recognize the marriages. This infringed on the plaintiffs' fundamental right of marriage, and denied them the equal protection of the law, all in violation of the Fourteenth Amendment.

A lawsuit needs to be "served" on the defendants. Bill knew Tennessee Attorney General Robert "Bob" Cooper. They had both practiced law in Nashville for years, and their fathers had served together as members of the Tennessee Supreme Court from 1974 through 1990. So when Bill called Bob Cooper, he readily agreed to allow Bill to come to his office and serve the papers personally. It was the duty of the Attorney General to respond for the state on behalf of all defendants. The case thus began with courtesy among the lawyers, and that courtesy continued until the case was finished.

The case was assigned to US District Judge Aleta Trauger. She would be the first judge to rule on the validity of Tennessee's nonrecognition laws. Within thirty days, the state filed an answer denying that the plaintiffs were entitled to any relief. The state asserted, among various defenses, that Tennessee law properly denied recognition to the plaintiffs' marriages.

The next move was up to the plaintiffs. A series of long conference calls began for the plaintiffs' legal team. Plaintiffs had many choices. They could engage in a "discovery" process involving depositions and written questions that each side could exchange. They could move for summary judgment, asking the Court to enter judgment without a trial because the questions were, arguably, purely legal issues. Another option would be to ask the Court to enter a preliminary injunction. A preliminary injunction would block Tennessee from enforcing its nonrecognition laws.

As primarily business lawyers, we cautioned against requesting a preliminary injunction. Courts place a very high burden on plaintiffs seeking preliminary injunctions and our business litigation experience had shown us numerous examples of plaintiffs stumbling at the outset of a case by being unsuccessful in seeking a preliminary injunction. In our experience, it was the quickest way to turn momentum against a plaintiff who otherwise had a meritorious case. However, the NCLR members of the team pointed out to us that this was unlike a business case and that we were shouldering the cause of not just our plaintiff couples, but all same-gender couples in Tennessee. Plus, we had a hook: Val and Sophy were expecting a baby in March, and both parents wanted to be listed on the birth certificate. If we got the injunction, the state would have to list both parents; without the injunction, it would be unlawful since the marriage would be deemed void. We were persuaded that moving for a preliminary injunction was the right decision.

The motion for a preliminary injunction was filed on November 19, 2013, and the state responded with a brief asking the Court to decline to issue an injunction. Time passed, and we were getting anxious for a ruling. The legal team filed a "motion to ascertain status": basically a letter to the judge asking her to tell us where things stood. Judge Trauger wrote back to the lawyers in the case almost immediately: "The Plaintiffs' Motion to Ascertain Status of the Case is GRANTED. The parties are informed that the court is working on the decision in this case."

Two days later, on March 14, 2014, Judge Trauger issued an order granting the plaintiffs' motion for a preliminary injunction. One of the criteria for granting such a motion is that the Court must find that the plaintiffs have a "likelihood of success on the merits." In other words, the Court makes an initial ruling that the plaintiffs are more likely than not to win the case. Judge Trauger's opinion went even further. It recited the stories of each of the plaintiff couples, in detail, with emphasis on the harm done to each couple by the state's refusal to recognize their marriage.

In evaluating whether Tennessee's nonrecognition laws should be invalidated, Judge Trauger recounted the string of cases after *Windsor* that had invalidated such laws around the country. She stated that "the evidence shows that the plaintiffs are suffering dignitary and practical harms that cannot be resolved through monetary relief. The state's refusal to recognize the plaintiffs' marriages de-legitimizes their relationships, degrades them in their interactions with the state, causes them to suffer public indignity, and invites public and private discrimination and stigmatization." Judge Trauger gave particular weight to Val and Sophy's upcoming birth, to Thom and Ijpe's marriage that was "on" when they were on the military base and "off" when they left it, and to the harm to Matt and Johno's children "during their developing years from the stigmatization and denigration of their family relationship."

Judge Trauger concluded: "At some point in the future, likely with the benefit of additional precedent from circuit courts and, perhaps, the Supreme Court, the court will be asked to make a final ruling on the plaintiffs' claims. At this point, all signs indicate that, in the eyes of the United States Constitution, the plaintiffs' marriages will be placed on an equal footing with those of heterosexual couples and that proscriptions against same-sex marriage will soon become a footnote in the annals of American history." We had won.

Back in Knoxville, Val and Sophy's baby was born. The injunction meant that, at least pending a change in the Court's ruling, their marriage was now valid and had to be recognized by the state of Tennessee. With Regina's help, both Val and Sophy were listed on the birth certificate as parents. It was the first time a same-gender couple had been officially listed as parents on a Tennessee birth certificate. A few weeks later, Bill visited Jay at law school in Knoxville, and Regina had a Sunday brunch with Bill, Jay and Jesse, and Val, Sophy, and the baby. There was champagne.

Under federal law, the grant of a preliminary injunction is immediately appealable to the US Court of Appeals without having to await the conclusion of the case in the district court. Tennessee filed an appeal from Judge Trauger's order, and the Court of Appeals issued an order staying the preliminary injunction. After that stay, Tennessee could once again enforce its nonrecognition laws.

Courts of Appeals are divided into circuits, and Tennessee falls into the Sixth Circuit, consisting of Tennessee, Kentucky,

Ohio, and Michigan. Federal appeals from those states all go to the Sixth Circuit, which is based in Cincinnati, Ohio. As it turned out, marriage equality cases from Kentucky, Ohio, and Michigan were all being appealed to the Sixth Circuit in the spring of 2014. The cases from Tennessee and Ohio were marriage recognition cases; the cases from Kentucky and Michigan also included rulings that required states to issue marriage licenses to same-gender couples. The plaintiffs in all four states had won their cases at the trial court level.

The Sixth Circuit issued an order putting all four cases (Tennessee, Kentucky, Ohio, and Michigan) on a similar oral argument schedule. While each set of plaintiffs and defendants in the four cases would file their own briefs and the cases would remain separate, they would be argued on the same day, back-to-back. Oral argument was set for August 6, 2014.

Meanwhile, other marriage-equality cases were being decided at a fast pace around the country. Many federal trial courts had ruled in favor of marriage equality, and circuit courts were beginning to follow suit. As the appeal progressed in the Sixth Circuit, no federal court had upheld state nonrecognition laws.

Tennessee's legal team worked on its briefs and began to reach out to the plaintiffs' lawyers from the other Sixth Circuit states. Decisions would have to be made about strategy, and it was critical that the effort be as united and coordinated as possible, given that the cases had originated differently. The legal teams from Tennessee, Kentucky, and Ohio met in Nashville, at our offices, on July 31, 2014. There were more than twenty lawyers in the meeting. The entire day was spent practicing, discussing, and worrying about the upcoming oral arguments. Bill would make the argument for the Tennessee plaintiffs.

That September, Jay Harbison and Jesse Ford were married. Our friend and newly confirmed Federal District Court Judge Pam Reeves officiated. Echoes of our marriage-equality case were present for the event, both because Jay and Jesse cared so much, and because Judge Reeves (like most of Tennessee's legal community) was aware of the significance of the pending litigation. In the program that Jay and Jesse prepared for the guests, the two of them expressed their happiness and joy on the occasion of their wedding, but also wrote that they were saddened that not all people in our country could yet share the joys of getting married—a pointed reminder that the case was by no means over, and that its outcome was far from certain.

The day before the arguments in the Sixth Circuit were to be heard, Bill drove to Cincinnati with Scott and John. Phil had a family engagement he could not miss. The night before the argument, we met with Abby, Regina, and Maureen. Shannon and Chris from NCLR joined us. It was a nerve-racking night.

The next morning, most of the lawyers met for breakfast at our hotel, and then walked together to the Sixth Circuit courthouse. Protesters, both for and against marriage equality, stood along the way. As we passed by, Abby said to the crowd: "We're from Tennessee, and we're going to win. We're making history."

The Sixth Circuit had set aside most of the day for the four cases. We met our plaintiffs, who had all come for the argument, and together found our way to the large courtroom where the Court would hear arguments. Although the room was full, there were seats for every lawyer from all four states, and for all plaintiffs, who had been given tickets to ensure that everyone could be present. Security was extremely tight; officers with dogs roamed the courtroom as people gathered.

The arguments would be made back-to-back in all four cases, starting in the early afternoon. Each case would begin with the state's attorney arguing for reversal of the trial court decision, and then with that state's plaintiff's attorney arguing to uphold the decision. A panel of three judges would decide the case. The Sixth Circuit had assigned Judges Sutton, Cook, and Daughtrey as the panel.

Tennessee's case was argued last, so Bill had a chance to listen to arguments in the first three cases. Each of the states argued that its laws restricting marriage to one man and one woman were supported by good reasons. It became clear that Judges Sutton and Cook believed that the laws could be upheld if they passed a legal test known as "rational basis." That is, if there were any rational state interests that could be served by the nonrecognition laws, the court would uphold them.

A theme that developed in the legal arguments that day was that it might be rational for states to take a wait-and-see approach with regard to marriage equality. A number of states recognized same-gender marriages, but a number did not. Judge Sutton, in particular, wondered aloud whether it might not be better in the long run for LGBTQ supporters to win hearts and minds by the political process, on a gradual basis, than to have a court force marriage equality on the states. Judge Daughtrey, on the other hand, asked the lawyer from Michigan whether he knew how long it had taken women to get the right to vote in the United States. He didn't know, and she told him that it had taken at least seventy-five years. She quipped that he should know that "in case you are ever on *Jeopardy*."

For the Tennessee case, the state's lawyer argued predictably that the Court should apply a rational basis standard of review and uphold the laws. The rational basis advanced by Tennessee involved the State's interest in procreation: opposite-gender couples could produce biological children, and same-gender couples could not. By restricting marriage to opposite-gender couples, the state could direct couples capable of reproducing into marriage, which would make society more stable and provide two-parent homes for children.

Bill's argument pointed out that the same interests in social stability and procreation would be furthered, not harmed, by recognizing the plaintiffs' marriages. It was obvious that Judge Daughtrey agreed. She asked Bill during the argument if he could explain the reasoning of the state. He answered, "for the life of me, I cannot."

After the argument, the Sixth Circuit panel took the case under advisement. It is standard practice for the Court to consider the arguments and to produce a written decision as soon as it can. There was little for the plaintiffs or their lawyers to do but wait. In September, the Seventh Circuit Court of Appeals decided a case in favor of marriage equality. This continued the nationwide trend of courts, after *Windsor*, finding that states had no legitimate interest in denying or failing to recognize the marriages of same-gender couples. As September and October passed, we felt hopeful that the trend in favor of marriage equality would continue.

Then, on November 6, 2014, the Sixth Circuit released its decision. Judges Sutton and Cook had voted to overturn the trial court decisions from all four states, including Tennessee. They found that the nonrecognition laws in all four states should be upheld, and served important state interests. Of considerable importance to the majority decision was the notion that voters should decide these matters on a state-by-state basis, and that federal courts should not take it upon themselves to make the decision. Judge Sutton's majority opinion concluded: "Better in this instance, we think, to allow change through the customary political processes, in which the people, gay and straight alike, become the heroes of their own stories by meeting each other not as adversaries in a court system but as fellow citizens seeking to resolve a new social issue in a fair-minded way."

Judge Daughtrey dissented. Her opinion strongly validated Judge Trauger's initial ruling. It was clear that she heard and understood the unique stories of the plaintiffs. Their individual rights under the Constitution, to be treated with equal protection and afforded due process, meant to her that the nonrecognition laws were unconstitutional. They served no legitimate purpose, rational or otherwise. They simply resulted in discrimination against gay and lesbian couples. As she noted in her opening paragraph: "In point of fact, the real issue before us concerns what is at stake in these...cases for the individual plaintiffs and their children, and what should be done about it." Judge Daughtrey characterized the majority opinion as having a view of the plaintiffs "as social activists who have somehow stumbled into federal court, inadvisably, when they should be out campaigning to win 'the hearts and minds' of Michigan, Ohio, Kentucky, and Tennessee voters to their cause....But these plaintiffs are not political zealots trying to push reform on their fellow citizens; they are committed same-sex couples, many of them heading up de facto families, who want to achieve equal status...and to be welcomed as fully legitimate parents at their children's schools. They seek to do this by virtue of exercising a civil right that most of us take for granted—the right to marry."

Despite the encouraging words from Judge Daughtrey, we had lost. Our clients were sad, but not completely surprised. Along with the lawyers, they had hoped that the case might end with the Sixth Circuit. Now we had to decide on the next step.

There were two legal paths left. One was to ask all of the judges on the Sixth Circuit to review the decision *en banc*. This would take time, and there was little assurance that the entire court would reach a different result. The other path was to appeal to the Supreme Court of the United States.

Most cases never reach the Supreme Court. The nine justices can decide only a finite number of appeals each year, and they select only the most significant cases for review. The process for asking the Court to take a case is to file a petition for a writ of certiorari, or a cert petition for short. This is essentially a brief explaining to the Court why a particular case is unique or significant enough for the Court to grant the appeal. If four justices vote to grant certiorari, the Court takes the case.

Our legal team had more conference calls after the Sixth Circuit decision, and reached out again to the plaintiffs' lawyers from the other Sixth Circuit states. Everyone quickly agreed that we should file a cert petition as quickly as possible. Taking the case to the Supreme Court was a daunting proposition. The odds of the Court taking a case are always long, and the work involved in presenting the case properly is immense.

Chris Stoll from NCLR then made a phone call. His Harvard Law School classmate Douglas Hallward-Driemier was at the Washington office of Ropes and Gray, a large international law firm. Doug had participated in many Supreme Court cases. Chris reached Doug and asked what he was doing that winter. Would he have time to join the legal team for Tennessee's marriage-equality case? Doug said yes right away.

Ropes and Gray would put a dozen lawyers on the case to help with the briefing. The entire Tennessee team remained involved, and the cert petition was the best work from every lawyer. It was truly a joint effort. Our cert petition was filed on November 14, 2014, along with cert petitions from Kentucky, Ohio, and Michigan.

One of the reasons that the Supreme Court takes a case is to resolve a conflict among the appellate circuit courts. The Sixth Circuit opinion was the first to find against marriage equality after *Windsor*, and it created a split with the other circuit courts that had ruled the other way. The circuit split was undoubtedly the reason that the Supreme Court granted all four cert petitions when it had previously denied other cert petitions posing the very same question prior to our loss in the Sixth Circuit. We found out on January 16, 2015. The cases from Tennessee, Kentucky, Ohio, and Michigan would be consolidated in the Supreme Court. Because Ohio's cert petition had been filed an hour earlier than ours, the case would bear the name of James Obergefell, the plaintiff in that case. The Court would decide two issues: whether the Fourteenth Amendment to the US Constitution required states to issue marriage licenses to persons of the same gender, and whether it also required states to recognize the marriages of same-gender couples who were married in another state.

It was time to write our briefs and tell our clients' stories to a third and final court, the United States Supreme Court.

John Farringer, Phil Cramer, Scott Hickman, Bill Harbison

10

THE CASE FOR MARRIAGE FOLLOWS US TO CHURCH

A s final edits on the Supreme Court brief were being made, God had plans at our church. On Monday, March 2, 2015, Phil received a call from Rev. Pam Hawkins, a dearly loved associate pastor. She had been appointed to our church four years earlier, and during that time had answered the call to be in ministry with and to LGBTQ persons who had responded to our church's hospitality.

Pam Hawkins shared with Phil that Doug and Frank, who had spoken so eloquently before the administrative board in 2012, were going to avail themselves of the Fourth Circuit Court of Appeals' decision striking down the same-gender marriage prohibitions within that circuit, which included the neighboring state of North Carolina. It was a five-hour drive from Nashville to the North Carolina state line. After years of waiting, Frank and Doug would legally wed, and they wanted their pastor, Rev. Hawkins, to officiate the ceremony.

The legal battle that we had been compelled by our faith formed at our church and that had brought us to the Supreme Court was now returning full circle to our faith community. Phil had previously scheduled a special session of the executive committee of the church's administrative board for the following evening on March 3, 2015, to plan for the potential that requests would be made of our church's staff and for its facilities in the event the Supreme Court ruled in favor of marriage equality. We thought we had at least three months to plan. Instead, we had three days. Frank and Doug were to be married on March 6.

Phil and Rev. Hawkins informed the executive team of the news of the impending nuptials. Every leader around the table at the meeting that evening firmly and unequivocally supported Rev. Hawkins in her decision. And the church leadership decided that we would stand by all of our clergy as they answered God's call and heeded their ordination vows, regardless of whether it was in conformity or conflict with *The Book of Discipline of The United Methodist Church.* The church leaders also knew that this moment would be

a defining one for our church, much like the decision faced by the church in 1962, when deciding whether to accept a person of color into membership of the church. Again, King's words loomed large over our deliberations. We decided as a group that we would approach this moment out of love and celebration instead of fear.

After informing the church's leadership, Rev. Hawkins informed her district superintendent and bishop of her intentions. Because the wedding was to involve Frank, Doug, and their immediate family, Rev. Hawkins's involvement in the ceremony would lack any firsthand witnesses, at least those of the mind-set to submit a complaint against her. However, Pam Hawkins took her actions openly and lovingly and prepared to accept the consequences. The question for our church was whether it would stand with Rev. Hawkins.

Unfortunately, a surprise snowstorm (which in the South is anything over two inches, and sometimes not even that) beset Tennessee, postponing Frank and Doug's plans to travel to North Carolina. The wedding would be scheduled for the following Friday. On Sunday, at the administrative board meeting, over which Phil was presiding, the lay leader, Bill Cooper, informed the board of the impending nuptials and Rev. Hawkins's intention to officiate the wedding. He reiterated the church's vision for nurturing, which aspired to have "every member of our faith family engaged in activities and relationships that address spiritual and human needs and offer opportunities for rest, rejuvenation, healing and growth." Bill spoke of the importance of his marriage and explained that the church's support and affirmation of his marriage was one of the key ways in which he and his wife, Amy, felt nurtured by this faith community. Bill then announced to the board:

As you know, the covenant of marriage has not always been available to all our members. However, with changes taking place throughout this country, that is now becoming a possibility. After waiting for literally decades, two of our members, Frank and Doug, have planned to become married in another state soon, as same-sex marriages are not currently recognized in the state of Tennessee. Earlier this week, Pam Hawkins, one of our clergy, informed us that after much prayer and discernment she will be heeding her call to provide pastoral support to this couple and participate in their wedding.

First, I hope you'll join me in celebrating this opportunity for our fellow church members and their family. This is a most fitting part of our focus on nurturing and also our further living into our welcoming creed's focus on Jesus' example of inclusive love, care, and intentional hospitality with persons of every race, ethnicity, age, sexual orientation, gender identity, marital status, faith story, physical or mental ability, economic status, or political perspective.

Second, I want to discuss with you briefly the implications of this decision for Pam and for our church. We recognize that marriage is a sacred bond and the ultimate commitment between two persons. We also recognize that marriage has been defined differently at different points of time throughout human history and the history of The United Methodist Church. We recognize that Methodists throughout the world are not of one mind with respect to same-gender marriage. Likewise, we recognize that our clergy have all taken vows to heed God's call to be in ministry with and to our faith community. We unconditionally love and support our clergy as they respond to God's call, recognizing that their path may lead them to be in conformity or conflict with the current official stance of The United Methodist Church on same-gender marriage.

Pam has been faithful in her commitment to our church members, to our church, and to our conference and transparent in her communication regarding her decision and her plans. She and [senior pastor] Ken [Edwards] have been in communication with Harriet Bryan, our District Superintendent, and Bill McAlilly, our Bishop. I have been moved by the compassionate and thoughtful approach that all our clergy and district and conference leaders have taken. We respect and appreciate District Superintendent Bryan's and Bishop McAlilly's leadership and discernment in these areas.

Pam was informed that if she participated in certain aspects of the wedding (the United Methodist word is *solemnize*), that a complaint would likely be filed with our bishop. These charges would result in a series of events, described in our *Book of Discipline*. It is my understanding that while the desired outcome of these events would be just resolution with mutual agreement from all parties, it is possible that judicial proceedings could occur, which could place Pam's credentials at risk. Pam is fully aware of these implications, and our district and conference leaders have been faithful in pastoring her in terms of her options and the implications.

As you consider your response to these events, we want to give you the opportunity to ask any questions you have and we will answer them with the best information we have. We simply can't predict every step, but I do assure you that your fellow leaders, including Phil Cramer, our Board Chair, Steve Deppen and the rest of the Staff Parish Relations Committee, our clergy, and I as your Lay Leader are committed to moving forward in a way consistent with our journey to date on these issues with thoughtful prayer, discernment, and ongoing dialogue. We have studied the process and outcomes in other jurisdictions to learn more, but recognize that no prior circumstances can completely inform the unique circumstances we will face together.

Many of you may have fears and concerns about what this might mean for Pam, our local church, and our larger church. I must confess that at times I have felt uncertain. I will tell you that as I have watched our local and connectional church leaders and clergy, I am more hopeful than fearful. At this point, we do not expect Pam's actions of pastoral care to affect other clergy in our church, nor do we anticipate adverse actions against the church. Staff Parish Relations is working closely with Pam to consider the implications of the possible complaint, the next steps, and our church's ongoing love, affirmation, and support for Pam and her ministry with and among us.

The administrative board was asked to pray for Frank, Doug, and their family along with Rev. Hawkins and the church's other clergy.

The bishop, having been provided a copy of this statement in advance, wrote a letter to the board, which was presented by the district superintendent who had come to attend the board meeting. The letter warned "that your conference leadership is not supportive of this decision" and explained that "regardless of the decisions you make as a congregation or your pastors make on behalf of your members, many of your sisters and brothers across the conference will have no capacity for understanding this decision." The bishop stated that "there will be, in the days to come, casualties in the body of Christ, both at Belmont and beyond" and urged that Rev. Hawkins not go forward with officiating the wedding. The bishop closed his letter stating: "I pray that you will all choose wisely."

The bishop's letter certainly garnered a reaction from those present. A resolution was introduced to voice, as a body, Belmont's affirmation and celebration of Frank and Doug. The resolution also asked the board to signal and affirm as a body the church's support for Rev. Hawkins and all of Belmont's clergy as they respond to God's call, recognizing that their path may lead them to be in conformity or conflict with the current official stance of The United Methodist Church on same-gender marriage. The resolution was overwhelmingly approved by a vote of 59 to 1. However, it was unclear what it meant at the time to fully support Rev. Hawkins and our clergy, but that would come into sharp focus over the forthcoming months.

The morning of Friday, March 6, 2015, was cool and rainy as the wedding party arrived at a park along the French Broad River outside of downtown Asheville. As Frank and Doug scoped out a scenic spot for the sharing of the vows, the rain stopped and the clouds began to clear. Phil had been asked to represent the church and co-officiate the wedding with Rev. Hawkins. It was the first wedding he had ever helped to officiate, and even more meaningful in light of the battle being simultaneously fought in the Supreme Court. The grooms each said "I do," and Rev. Hawkins signed the marriage license, making it official.

As Phil and Rev. Hawkins drove back to Nashville, Rev. Hawkins contacted her district superintendent and bishop to confirm that she had indeed officiated the wedding. While the marriage was legal in North Carolina, it was a chargeable offense against Rev. Hawkins under *The Book of Discipline of The United Methodist Church*. The bishop took action quickly. In a letter to Rev. Hawkins dated March 19, 2015, the bishop placed Rev. Hawkins on immediate leave requiring her to cease all "ministerial duties." The bishop, however, had apparently misconstrued his authority under paragraph ¶351 of *The Book of Discipline*, which addresses voluntary Spiritual and Formational Leave that a pastor, in conjunction with her local church's Staff-Parish Relations Committee, may *apply* to take, with the *permission* of both the local administrative board and the district superintendent. This leave could not be unilaterally imposed by a bishop or anyone else. Phil and the other lay leadership of Belmont immediately took action.

After Phil outlined the disciplinary mistakes in the suspension and walked the district superintendent through this analysis, word came back from the bishop's office that the suspension had been rescinded. However, the bishop also announced that he was suspending Rev. Hawkins under ¶363(1)(d) of the *Discipline*. Again, Phil pointed out that such a suspension could only be initiated upon the recommendation of the executive committee of the Board of Ordained Ministry. As such a recommendation had not been made, the bishop had again suspended Rev. Hawkins without due process. Rather than go before the executive committee of the Board of Ordained Ministry, the bishop again withdrew the suspension.

While the bishop's efforts to suspend Rev. Hawkins were successfully averted, Rev. Hawkins still had to endure the complaint process. Because that process is confidential, the details will not be published here. However, from the perspective of those of us who worked with Rev. Hawkins, the process took an extreme emotional and even physical toll on her. Without question, an example was being made of her. Throughout this time, our church and its lay leadership continued to stand with Rev. Hawkins. The bishop, however, took aim directly at the congregation's leadership. At one point, the prospect was raised of charges being made against the entire administrative board and the bishop accused the board of being "failed leaders."

Attempts were made to de-escalate the conflict. Well-respected leaders within the church met with the bishop to engage in faithful dialogue and Phil proposed to the bishop that the two meet to share their faith stories, break bread together, and learn about each other on a personal level. Perhaps by hearing each other's stories and perspective, Christian love and understanding might be factored into the situation. But adversarial roles were defined by the disciplinary complaint process, including the bishop's supervision of pastors and Phil's role on the administrative board in providing advice to Rev. Hawkins for that process. All parties obviously wished to avoid a church trial over solemnizing a same-gender marriage, and Rev. Hawkins eventually agreed to a suspension and other punitive measures in order to resolve the charges against her. The resolution was announced three days prior to Belmont's July 19, 2015, administrative board meeting. The meeting was standing room only, with Belmonters showing up to express support for Rev. Hawkins along with outrage and disappointment with some leaders of the Tennessee Conference. Belmonters took up a fund to support Rev. Hawkins during her suspension, which was raised literally overnight. It would not be the last time the church came together to support marriage equality.

Indeed, within a month of Rev. Hawkins's suspension, a multi-generational group within the congregation with broad perspectives and beliefs, was tasked by the board to draft petitions for inclusion at 2016 General Conference, the following year. The petitions all addressed inclusion of LGBTQ persons in *The Book of Discipline* and sought the recognition of all marriages regardless of the genders of the couple. The petitions sought to eliminate all references to "heterosexual marriage" and to delete the prohibition on the participation of clergy in marriage ceremonies between persons of the same gender. The petitions were adopted in full by the church and circulated to other United Methodist churches and members around the world, hundreds of whom joined our church's petitions. Our church, like many others, had taken the fight for marriage equality from its local church to the worldwide denomination.

11

CULMINATION OF THE JOURNEY TO THE SUPREME COURT

The Tennessee team would file briefs in the Supreme Court for its plaintiffs, and similar briefs would be filed by the plaintiffs from Kentucky, Ohio, and Michigan. But the Court made clear that the cases were consolidated into one single case at the Supreme Court level. They would permit a total of four lawyers to argue: one representative for the plaintiffs and one for the defendant states on the right to marry, and one representative for the plaintiffs and one for the defendant states on marriage recognition.

The first issue, on the right to marry, was presented by the Kentucky and Michigan cases. The second issue, on marriage recognition, was presented by Tennessee and Ohio. It made sense, therefore, to have a plaintiffs' lawyer from either the Kentucky or Michigan teams to argue the first issue in the Supreme Court, and to have a plaintiffs' lawyer from either Tennessee or Ohio argue the marriage recognition issue. But how could we agree?

Tennessee and Ohio agreed to have what we came to call a "moot off" to select our oral advocate. A moot court is a mock or practice legal argument. Our team offered Doug, from the Ropes and Gray firm, who was the most experienced Supreme Court practitioner on any of the state legal teams. Ohio's lead lawyer was Al Gerhardstein, who had argued for James Obergefell at the Sixth Circuit. After the moot, Al graciously agreed that it should be Doug to make our Supreme Court argument.

It was now up to Kentucky and Michigan to select their oral advocate. This process was more fraught. It is understandable that many of the lawyers who had fought for marriage equality would want to argue the case in the Supreme Court. After a moot court at the University of Michigan, a consensus candidate emerged in Mary Bonauto, who had been added to Michigan's legal team. Mary had argued the case for marriage equality in the Supreme Judicial Court of Massachusetts, and was a highly revered LGBTQ rights advocate. She would argue the first issue, about the right to marry, in the Supreme Court.

The oral argument in the Supreme Court was set for Tuesday, April 28, 2015. The four lawyers from our firm—Bill, Phil, Scott, and John—went to Washington a week before the hearing date. There would be two moot court sessions in Washington. One was at the Howard University Law School on the Wednesday before the actual argument. Before the moot court, the director of the Howard program drove home the significance of the marriage equality case, explaining that it was the most significant civil rights case that Howard had mooted since the 1954 landmark decision in *Brown v. Board of Education*, abolishing the "separate but equal" doctrine that had for decades permitted public school racial segregation. The second moot court would take place two days later at Georgetown Law School. All of the plaintiffs' lawyers from all four states were there for both moot court sessions. Distinguished lawyers, law professors, and LGBTQ advocates attended and judged the arguments. All of us had a chance to comment, think of questions, and strategize.

Mary and Doug were flooded with suggestions. What if a member of the Court asked whether our position would also require recognition of polygamous marriages? What about incestuous marriages? After the actual moot courts, there were meetings at Doug's offices at Ropes and Gray to revise, refine, and try to perfect the best arguments.

The core of our legal team was still Abby, Regina, and Maureen. The four of us from Sherrard & Roe, with Abby, Regina, and Maureen, found a Chinese restaurant after the Howard moot court. They served a drink called an Angry Bastard that Bill and Regina favored. We went back to that restaurant four more times while we were in Washington. It became a point of reference—and togetherness—for our group.

Over the weekend, John returned home to Nashville to be with his family, and Phil made a quick trip to Baltimore to spend time with his parents. Bill and Scott stayed in Washington for the weekend, where they visited the memorials for Martin Luther King Jr. and Franklin Roosevelt. They also spent most of a day at the Holocaust Museum.

Bill's wife, Patty, would join the group on Sunday. Bill and Patty had met as students at Harvard Law School in the 1970s, and were married in Patty's home state of Ohio in 1980 after they graduated. They then moved to Bill's hometown in Nashville, where their Ohio marriage has been recognized by Tennessee for thirty-seven years and counting.

On Monday, all the lawyers from our team were back together in Washington. Doug and Mary had been preparing for the argument all weekend. Doug had asked Scott to join him on Monday for a long walk and a chance to talk about the argument. We gathered at our Chinese restaurant that night, and nervously waited.

The next morning was clear and chilly. The plaza before the Supreme Court, and the sidewalks all around, were packed with people. Most seemed to be people protesting against marriage equality. Posters and signs denounced sin and called homosexuality an abomination. We walked into the courthouse, receiving a fair share of denouncements for what we were doing. Through it all, Abby smiled and told everyone, "We're from Tennessee, and we're going to win. We're making history."

The argument began at 10:30 that morning in a packed courtroom. The US government had decided to join the plaintiffs in asking the Court to overturn the Sixth Circuit decision and rule for marriage equality. Mary argued first on behalf of the plaintiffs. The Solicitor General for the United States also argued. State attorneys from Michigan and Tennessee presented the case for the states, asking the court to affirm the Sixth Circuit's decision. During the oral argument, a protestor had snuck into the courtroom and began shouting; he was forcefully dragged out of the courtroom by the US Marshals, although his voice continued to reverberate through the courtroom as he was dragged through the outer hallways.

When it was time for Doug to argue, many of the questions had been asked and he was allowed to speak with few interruptions. He took time to tell the stories of Val and Sophy, Matthew and Johno, and Thom and Ijpe. Each couple had a unique story of being married, moving to Tennessee, and then having their state refuse to recognize their marriages for any purpose. Doug's telling of their stories was the end of the argument that day.

When the argument ended, courtroom deputies began to direct everyone out of the courthouse. Our legal team managed to meet with all six of our clients, and together we walked down the front steps of the Supreme Court. All the clients were in tears. Their stories had been told.

The National Center for Lesbian Rights had arranged for a late lunch for the Tennessee team in a private room of a nearby restaurant. All the clients and lawyers gathered there for the afternoon. Many people gave toasts, and there was an atmosphere of hope as well as apprehension. As speeches were being made, Doug leaned over to us and whispered, "This is why we went to law school."

We were now back to waiting to see what the Court would decide. May passed, and most of June, without a decision. The Supreme Court does not give advance notice of when it will release opinions. Toward the end of June, we knew that a decision was imminent.

On Friday, June 26, Bill was in state court at a motion hearing. At about 9:15 a.m. another lawyer in the courthouse announced that the Supreme Court had ruled in favor of marriage equality. As Bill left the courthouse, he met Phil on the courthouse steps. Phil was on his way into court for a case and had just received a phone call from his wife, Anna, telling him the exciting news. It was a fitting way to learn of the decision from one's spouse. Our meeting on the courthouse steps was unexpected—but we shared a moment of elation before the rest of that day played out.

Chapter 11

The ruling in *Obergefell* was, not surprisingly, a 5 to 4 decision by the Supreme Court. Justice Kennedy authored the majority opinion, and there were strong dissents from Justices Roberts, Scalia, Thomas, and Alito. We had always suspected that Justice Kennedy would provide the deciding vote. At the argument, it had appeared obvious that Justices Ginsburg, Breyer, Sotomayor, and Kagan were supportive of marriage equality.

Justice Kennedy's opinion rested on two major premises: marriage is a fundamental right, and it is a violation of due process and equal protection for states to grant that right only to heterosexual couples. He wrote: "The nature of injustice is that we may not always see it in our own times. The generations that wrote and ratified the Bill of Rights and the Fourteenth Amendment did not presume to know the extent of freedom in all of its dimensions, and so they entrusted to future generations a character protecting the right of all persons to enjoy liberty as we learn its meaning."

Underpinning the Court's ruling is the fundamental importance of human dignity. The right to personal choice in marriage is "inherent in the concept of individual autonomy." A "two-person union [is] unlike any other in its importance to the committed individuals." Justice Kennedy summed up the case: "No union is more profound than marriage, for it embodies the highest ideals of love, fidelity, devotion, sacrifice, and family.... [The challengers] ask for equal dignity in the eyes of the law. The constitution grants them that right."

Bill got back to our firm's offices about 9:30 on that Friday morning of June 26. He was on the phone with the office of the Tennessee Attorney General. While the case was pending, General Cooper had left office and a new Attorney General, Herbert Slatery, had been appointed. Bill and members of the Attorney

General's office discussed what would occur in the aftermath of the opinion. The courtesy among the lawyers that had marked the beginning of the case continued through the end. Tennessee would do the right thing: both Governor Haslam and Attorney General Slatery issued formal press releases explaining that, although they were disappointed with the Supreme Court's ruling, it was now the law of the land, and state officials should immediately honor the ruling. Marriage licenses were issued around the state that morning, and by noon same-gender weddings were being performed in Tennessee—and the world changed.

12

CULMINATION OF OUR CHURCH'S JOURNEY

After the Supreme Court decision and the submission of the eight petitions to General Conference, our congregation eagerly awaited the 2016 General Conference. We were optimistic that our petitions would be adopted by General Conference. That did not happen. Instead, a delay was proposed in the form of a special commission whose work would not likely be addressed until at least 2019, which would place our local church and LGBTQ persons attending Belmont in limbo. For some within our church, the refusal of the denomination to fully recognize their human dignity and basic sacred worth was the last straw. They had come back to church with the promise of the church's welcoming statement but now felt betrayed by the larger church's decision. They left the church.

For many of us who remained at the church, we recognized the need to take action; again, the fierce urgency of now from Martin Luther King Jr. rang in our ears. The church commissioned its own task force to more fully understand the options before Belmont and the potential ramifications of those options. The task force sought to fully understand the range of options available to the congregation and the risks associated with those options. In so doing, our church was not unlike any other congregation attempting to explore alternatives and gather information about them. To be faithful, however, all options needed to be evaluated, which ranged from expectantly waiting for the next three years to leaving the denomination. As with our practice of law, we are obliged to advise clients on all options available to them, even those that may be far afield or unadvisable. We know that other congregations throughout the country (and beyond) and across many different denominations have engaged in similar undertakings.

Phil was asked to head up the task force; and unlike the denomination's commission, the group would complete its work in a matter of weeks.

The task force considered numerous primary and secondary sources in undertaking its research, including *The Book of Discipline*, Council of Bishop's Proposal from General Conference 2016, Record of General Conference 2016, interviews with and firsthand accounts from various delegates to and attendees at General Conference 2016, relevant Judicial Council rulings/decisions, input and involvement from every pastoral staff member of BUMC, interview with the district superintendent, statements of Bishop McAlilly and the Board of Trustees of the Tennessee Annual Conference of The United Methodist Church, Belmont's legal records, including deed and property appraisals, Belmont's wedding policy, prior decision-making processes utilized by Belmont, legal case law derived from fifty-state legal searches, numerous print sources—articles, news reports, FAQs, church websites, blogs, and other firsthand and secondhand sources—individual case studies from other churches throughout Nashville and the Southeast, and conversations with both the legal team and executive director of Reconciling Ministries Network.

The task force's goal was to gather information so that the congregation and its decision-makers could make informed decisions about next steps. Much like how a lawyer attempts to help a client separate myth from reality and more appropriately to quantify risk, the task force dug deep to evaluate even those options that its individual members strongly disfavored. However, members of the task force had seen over the years how misinformation or mistaken assumptions had unduly influenced past decisions. Of course, that was not limited to just the church. The Supreme Court has all but admitted that its past decisions denying equal protection to LGBTQ individuals were based on mistaken assumptions regarding the facts and the law.

Within our church, we had witnessed a common misconception that Belmont could lose its church property if same-gender weddings were performed on premises. Pursuant to the "trust provision" of *The Book of Discipline*, the church owns its property in putative trust for the annual conference. The task force's research revealed, however, that this does not mean that the church property may be taken by the conference if, for example, there were same-gender weddings in the sanctuary or the church endorsed a gay candidate for ministry. There is no basis in *The Book of Discipline* or in legal precedent for the church's property to be taken or for the congregation to be removed from the church grounds under such a scenario. Moreover, the task force's research confirmed that there was no desire for or practical risk of such an event for so long as Belmont continued to be a United Methodist congregation.

The task force also found no precedent or grounds for "charges" by the bishop or any viable complaint against any of our church's pastoral staff as a result of same-gender weddings occurring on church property in which the pastor does not participate. The one possible exception would be the senior pastor, who could conceivably be charged under ¶2702.1(d) of *The Book of Discipline* for "disobedience to the order and discipline of The United Methodist Church" or pursuant to the senior pastor's obligation for administration of the church. However, the task force's research did not reveal a single instance nationwide in which any pastor was charged under this section for a same-gender wedding occurring on church grounds in which the pastor did not participate. The task force's research also suggested that such a complaint or charge against the senior pastor under such circumstances would both suffer from several legal infirmities and represent an inequitable application of *The Book of Discipline*, which also prohibits, for example, re-baptisms on church grounds or failure to keep church records off-campus, and yet there is substantial precedent that such events have and do regularly occur throughout the district, conference, and denomination.

The task force observed that if there were to be a decision to perform a same-gender wedding at Belmont, nothing in the wedding policy or *The Book of Discipline* required that a pastoral staff member publicize weddings held at the church to the broader congregation or alert the district or conference leadership of each wedding performed at Belmont. The task force's research discovered that many bishops require that any complaints made against a pastor for performing a same-gender wedding be submitted by a person with firsthand knowledge.

Finally, the task force noted that as our church had moved forward in our journey toward inclusiveness, the church had experienced tremendous growth and vitality. For example, more new members joined the church in 2015 than in any previous year in recent history. Nearly every age group had experienced growth and implemented vital new ministries, including our ministries with children, confirmands, youth, young adults, and senior adults. There were more new pledges to the operating campaign for 2016 than in the past twenty years.

However, the task force's report to church leadership was met with skepticism by some and downright distrust by others. In retrospect, it is now apparent why: the task force had focused on empirical data, legal research, and risk analysis. While this was the charge of the task force, it was a departure from the focus on human dignity and the elevation of personal narratives that had previously brought the church together. Indeed, most of the work of the task force would never be disseminated to the broader church or even the administrative board itself. In frustration, Phil would step down from chairing the task force.

Fortunately, Belmont would soon be refocused. At our annual All Church Retreat, Rev. Emily Townes, dean of the Vanderbilt Divinity School, was the featured speaker. Dean Townes warned of the dangers of gradualism as a call to action. She explained the difference between two different four-letter words in our church: "love" and "nice." "Love" is what makes us a church community; "nice" is what typically prevents us from fulfilling God's will. It was a powerful narrative and one that rang true. After all, Jesus loved everyone, but he was not nice to everyone; indeed, he saved many of his harshest words for those whom he loved and to whom he was closest. The church would give Dean Townes a standing ovation at the closing session. It was not lost on anyone how we could applaud Dean Townes and thank her for spending her time with us yet somehow we would deny Dean Townes and her same-gender partner the opportunity to be married at our church.

So church leadership went back to our congregation. On October 12, 2016, another church-wide discernment effort began. Church leadership recognized that for many in our church family, waiting two years for the Bishop's Commission to complete its work and for any subsequent action to be taken at the denominational level was simply not acceptable. At the same time, church leadership recognized that there are many in our church family who were concerned about making decisions that placed us in conflict with the denomination's rules and policies.

The church board therefore sought to hear from all church members about where they heard God's call in relation to same-gender weddings in our church or performed by our clergy, or both. Two long-time Belmonters agreed to facilitate the listening process over the course of several weeks. Part of the reason for having further listening sessions was that in the time since our last church-wide listening process, several new persons had joined our church family, and the church leadership wanted to ensure that all members had a chance to share their hopes and dreams for the church, as well as their concerns. Again, it was important to hear everyone's narrative.

The listening sessions were fast-tracked and completed within two months. A team then sought to make sense of what had been shared. The results reflected the collective experience of having listened to one another. Belmonters did not want to simply wait. They wanted action. They wanted to advocate for change within the denomination while moving forward with change within the local church. A majority of Belmonters supported both affiliating with Reconciling Ministries Network while also opening up the church's sanctuary for same-gender weddings despite the wording of *The Book of Discipline*. Interestingly, Belmonters rejected both the notion of discontinuing all weddings at the church (which would have complied with *The Book of Discipline* while ensuring that no one was treated unequally) and the idea of having same-gender weddings occur at an off-site facility (which raised the ugly connotation of separate but equal from past times).

Nonetheless, church leadership found themselves at an impasse. Despite the data collected by both the task force and the church-wide listening process, church leadership was uncertain about next steps. The bishop had taken notice of our discernment process and warned of consequences. Some of us wanted to move forward, while others of us, believing in the same end goals, favored a more cautious and gradual approach. We then realized that we had changed our focus to data and discernment rather than returning to first principles. And with a return to those principles, the impasse was broken.

Taking a step back, we realized that our time of discernment and prayer revealed that we share common values, common hopes, and common understandings of God's will. We all believe in the power and grace of our faith community. We all love our church and every member of our church. We all believe that God loves every member of our church and created each of us in the image of God. We all want our faith community to remain strong and stay together; we believe that the sum of our faith community is greater than its individual parts. We all believe that God's love is transformative and that our love of one another has the power to transform. We all know that God's will calls us to love another as God loves us. We all believe in full inclusion and that our church should not discriminate based on sexual orientation; we hear Christ calling Belmont to be a place where every person is fully included and welcomed fully into the life of this congregation. We all find joy in bringing joy to one another and to others. We all value diversity and believe our differences make us stronger as an expression of Christ's body and as a witness to the all-encompassing love of God we have come to know in Jesus Christ. We all remain committed to our church family and to Belmont United Methodist Church. We all love and support our clergy and respect their call to service, even when it may conflict with *The Book of Discipline*'s language regarding human sexuality. And we are a united faith family that is not just accepting, but welcoming and celebrating all persons regardless of sexual orientation.

By focusing on such principles, a path forward emerged. At an All Church Retreat several years ago, our leader told the modern-day parable of the hymn. Just as in every family, members have different tastes and different preferences—not every hymn in the hymnal is likely your favorite. But it is probably the favorite of someone, perhaps the very person sitting next to you. And the lesson we learned at All Church Retreat was to take joy in singing every hymn, not just those that you like, because chances are that whatever hymn may be your least favorite, is someone else's most favorite. And by joining together in singing that hymn, we collectively bring joy to that fellow member and through his or her joy, each of us experiences joy.

So that everyone can have a chance to sing their favorite hymn and so that the hymnal is available to all, the church created its own path forward. We would encourage and support intentional actions by our church as a united body to actively advocate for change, including petitioning the Commission on a Way Forward, our resident bishop, our conference delegates to General Conference, and the Southeast Jurisdiction, proposing solutions or other reasonable means to influence the outcome and achievement of our objective. We would support the ordination of all persons called and gifted for pastoral ministry regardless of their sexual orientation. We would support our clergy who individually feel called to perform same-gender weddings. We would vote as an entire congregation to affiliate with Reconciling Ministries Network to take a take a public stand and let all know that they are welcome at our church. And we would ensure that our wedding policy was inclusive and would not discriminate based on the genders of those seeking to be wed.

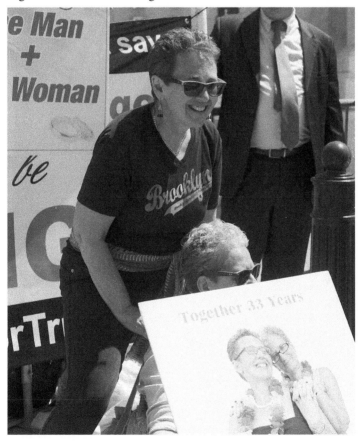

13

LESSONS FROM CHURCH CONFLICT AND COURTROOM CONTESTS

Our book about making a case for marriage in the courts and in the church ends where it began: baptism. Bill's three children (Jay, Clare, and Jane Coleman) and Phil's three children (Caroline, Lucy, and Alice) were all baptized before witnesses of our faith community. When they were baptized we made the following solemn promise:

> On behalf of the whole Church, I ask you:
> Do you renounce the spiritual forces of wickedness,
> reject the evil powers of this world,
> and repent of your sin?

I do.

> Do you accept the freedom and power God gives you
> to resist evil, injustice, and oppression
> in whatever forms they present themselves?

I do.

Our whole congregation then took this oath in support of our families:

> Do you, as Christ's body, the Church,
> reaffirm both your rejection of sin
> and your commitment to Christ?
>
> **We do.**
>
> Will you nurture one another in the Christian faith and life
> and include these persons now before you in your care?
>
> **With God's help we will proclaim the good news**
> **and live according to the example of Christ.**
> **We will surround these persons**
> **with a community of love and forgiveness,**
> **that they may grow in their trust of God,**
> **and be found faithful in their service to others.**
> **We will pray for them,**
> **that they may be true disciples**
> **who walk in the way that leads to life.**

Our journeys to the US Supreme Court and within our church were grounded in these solemn promises. Not only the promises that we took to resist evil, injustice, and oppression in whatever forms they present themselves but also the covenant embraced by the entire congregation to surround us with a community of love and forgiveness to walk in the way that leads to life.

Likewise, when we each joined our church as members, we promised "to be loyal to Christ." This pledge of loyalty is not an oath to any human institution, law, or book. That would be idolatry. Instead, we profess loyalty to Christ. This instilled upon us the obligation and the responsibility to question laws and customs, whether they be civil or church, that deprive equality and dignity from the voiceless and powerless.

Our journeys to the United States Supreme Court and within our congregation revealed two basic truths. First, narratives are important. As two of the team of attorneys for gay and lesbian couples, our job was to provide a platform for their voices to be heard. We were storytellers for people who are often silenced. And while we told these stories against a legal backdrop and within the context of the law, at the end of the day the stories of our plaintiffs and countless others like them were what ultimately swayed five US Supreme Court justices, especially Justice Anthony Kennedy. It was no coincidence that Doug, our Supreme Court counsel, used his precious rebuttal time during oral argument to refocus the Court on the human narratives instead of the legal dogma.

We experienced the same thing at our local church. Over the countless years of discussion and discernment, the stories of individual members in a particular congregation served to change more hearts and minds than any deep dive into scripture, church doctrine, or the law. The expression of stories brought both understanding and empathy. It also allowed individual church members to connect in a deeper and more meaningful manner to form a stronger faith community.

The second and related lesson learned from both experiences was the importance of focusing on human dignity. Justice Kennedy's ultimate decision did not rest on a recitation of history or a legalistic articulation of the proper standard of review. It rested on the basic and universal principle of human dignity. According to Justice Kennedy, the same-gender couples had asked only "for equal dignity in the eyes of law." Justice Kennedy explained that "there is dignity in the bond between two men or two women who seek to marry" and that marriage itself "always has promised nobility and dignity to all persons, without regard to their station in life."

So too within our church, despite disagreement over scripture and church law, there emerged universal agreement over the sacred worth and dignity of all of God's children. Such recognition brought the church together to welcome all persons and to celebrate all persons, regardless of sexual orientation. By focusing on the sacred worth of individuals as opposed to singling out certain persons, the church was able to move together as a single body committed to hospitality to all. And once that threshold was crossed, the narrative changed from us versus them to all of us together.

Toward that end, it was the relationships that we formed and persons whose paths we crossed that will endure for us. It is the wonderful group of plaintiffs—Val and Sophy, Thom and Ijpe, and Matt and Johno—whom we had the privilege of representing. We still think often of our plaintiffs. This courageous group of couples not only shared their stories with the world but they also welcomed us into their lives. We met their children. We spent time with them after the case at various venues throughout the United States. Although they have all now moved from Tennessee, they have left Tennessee a better and more welcoming place. We are forever grateful for how they touched our lives and trusted us with the privilege of telling their stories.

We also had the pleasure and privilege of working with a talented and diverse group of attorneys—Abby, Regina, Maureen, Scott, John, Shannon, David, Chris, and Doug. These were not attorneys with whom we had previously worked or in most cases even met. Yet, by the end of the lawsuit we count these attorneys among those to whom we are closest in the entire legal community. The bonds we formed have lasted well beyond the case. We have spent time in one another's homes. We have met one another's children. And we have worked with one another professionally and within the legal community. This is perhaps best exemplified by Bill and Abby, who worked to form a LGBT section of the Tennessee Bar Association, which Bill ushered in while president-elect of the bar association, with Abby serving as the inaugural chair.

The enduring relationships with fellow counsel are among the most meaningful reminders we have of our journey. Every June 26, all of us and our families get together to commemorate the Supreme Court opinion. And given the attention the case has received, we have been fortunate to be able to spend time with one another at various events in San Francisco (where NCLR is based), New York (where Joe Biden celebrated the success of Freedom to Marry), and Nashville (at the annual ACLU dinner).

One of our fondest memories was when Phil hosted a dinner for all of the attorneys and we were then invited to a celebration party at a local LGBTQ venue. Fittingly, Rev. Pam Hawkins, along with Frank and Doug, joined us for that celebration. It was a reminder to us of the dual worlds in which we had journeyed and the fact that our faith and faith community were always with us. In fact, it was our faith community that twice had us present at the church about the marriage equality case—first, while the case was pending in the Court of Appeals and then after the case had been decided by the Supreme Court. These opportunities to bring our legal work to our church reciprocated how our church had stood with us while we brought the case to court.

We do not profess to have all the answers to conflicts within our society and our churches. Our own stories are limited to our individual experiences within a single lawsuit and a single church. However, we have witnessed firsthand the power of storytelling and the universal bond of human dignity. We have watched how persons of differing backgrounds and perspectives came to understand and appreciate one another on a deep and personal level by simply listening to one another's stories. Stories cannot be debated and they cannot be disputed. They are true merely because they exist. Taking time to hear someone's story does two powerful things. First, it provides the person telling the story with an opportunity to be heard. Second, every story has an effect on the listener, especially when the story is one that is different from the listener's own experience. As attorneys and church leaders we found ourselves in the position of providing a platform and voice to those whose stories were being drowned out or never told at all.

The mere act of listening to a story can be transformative for both the listener and the teller of the story. By listening to a person's story, the listener recognizes the inherent dignity of the storyteller. And the storyteller receives this recognition of his or her dignity while also acknowledging the dignity of the listener to whom the story is told. Too often in our profession and even our church life, we get caught up in debates without pausing to listen to the narratives of those with whom we disagree. In so doing, we turn our focus away from the human dignity of those around us. In fact, we justify our conduct whether it be toward an opposing party, attorney, or fellow church member by attacking their position instead of taking a step back to listen to their narratives and recognize their basic human dignity.

In both the courtroom and the church, we have learned that common ground is almost never possible until adversaries truly listen to each other and mutually focus on human dignity as a guiding principle. At the French restaurant in Washington, we paused to reflect just before the Supreme Court arguments in April 2015. The couple at the next table became our friends and supporters for that night—without even exchanging names with us. But the four of us listened to one another during dinner. It was a memorable time.

CPSIA information can be obtained
at www.ICGtesting.com
Printed in the USA
LVHW01s0307220218
567477LV00003B/3/P

9 781501 858932